RAVE REVIEWS

"Tommy's raw honesty about his past struggles and journey to success resonated with me profoundly…I would highly recommend this story of growth to others who are seeking a courageous and authentic read."

ALEXIS QUINTAL
PR and Personal Branding Expert

"One of the most entertaining, honest and heartfelt books I've ever read. It will pull at your heartstrings as much as it will make you burst into laughter."

CHRIS ROLLINS
CEO Ripple Effect Leadership

"Once you peel back the layers of his story, you understand his journey, his can-do spirit and why he never gave up. It's inspirational for anyone with a challenging start in life."

MAUREEN FAMIANO
Media Expert, TEDx Speaker, Bestselling Author

This book is not just another rags-to-riches story; it's a flip-flops-to-foundations story. A lighthearted and serious story about overcoming adversity to build the framework of a successful life, while never forgetting where you came from.

JESSICA CASUCCI, ESQ.

BUILDING SUCCESS

BUILDING SUCCESS

A TOOLBOX FOR COMING OUT ON TOP

TOMMY WHITEHEAD

Copyright © 2024 by Tommy Whitehead

All rights reserved. This book or any portion thereof may not be reproduced or used in any manner whatsoever without the express written permission of the publisher except for the use of brief quotations in a book review.

Printed in the United States of America
First Printing, 2024

This book is based on true events. It reflects the author's present recollections of experiences over time. Some names and characteristics have been changed, some events have been compressed, and some dialogue has been recreated.

For an even bigger toolbox of success, visit the Building Success website:

Published by
TomCo Solutions
1211 Tech Blvd Ste 110
Tampa, FL 33619
www.TomCoSolutions.com

ISBN: 979-8-9886776-4-2 (Paperback)

DEDICATION

To my late mother and the unique traits that made us both different and the same. I gained an unyielding will from your example. Your spirit echoes in these pages and in my heart.

Sylvia Michelle Whitehead 12/29/66 – 08/22/22

CONTENTS

Foreword	1
CHAPTER ONE My Backpack Told Me I Was Poor	5
CHAPTER TWO That Time I Taught My Mom Algebra	15
CHAPTER THREE I Only Had to Panic for Two Hours	25
CHAPTER FOUR My Fake Self Showed Up for Work Today	37
CHAPTER FIVE Don't Take Advice from People Going the Wrong Direction	47
CHAPTER SIX I'm Not Your Interior Designer	55
CHAPTER SEVEN The Change Orders Can Kill You	65
CHAPTER EIGHT Know What Your Lunch is Worth	71
CHAPTER NINE Rich Dad, Poor Dad, Rebuilding Dad	79
CHAPTER TEN The Real Problems are Under the Drywall	89
CHAPTER ELEVEN Study the Hamburgers on Your Spreadsheet	95
CHAPTER TWELVE There is Power in Your Network	101

CHAPTER THIRTEEN
Just Because You're Forty Doesn't Mean You Know What You're Doing — 109

CHAPTER FOURTEEN
That Random Trivia is Good for More than Jeopardy — 117

CHAPTER FIFTEEN
Welp, That Shit's Gonna Fail — 121

CHAPTER SIXTEEN
There's More to Business Than Money — 127

CHAPTER SEVENTEEN
You Gotta Love Free Upgrades — 137

CHAPTER EIGHTEEN
Sometimes You Gotta Make Lemonade in the Bathtub — 143

CHAPTER NINETEEN
32 Boxes of M&M's is Exactly Enough — 151

CHAPTER TWENTY
Green is the Color of Disruptors — 155

Photo Album — 165

Acknowledgments — 173

About the Author — 177

FOREWORD

My first encounter with Tommy Whitehead was at a large networking event. I had been told so often about what a go-getter he was, but I'd heard that before about other people. That's why my first thought was, *We'll see if it lasts*. I'm happy to say I was wrong to doubt him. Not only has Tommy sustained his efforts in all areas of his life and work but he has improved them continuously, often taking quantum leaps daily, sometimes changing and pivoting hour by hour to ensure the best outcomes for his endeavors.

You might be saying, "So what? He's no different from all the other high achievers I've ever known, including myself." Possibly true, except Tommy is also a high achiever in all the areas that matter. I've never seen anyone outgive Tommy in the area of win/win solutions, and I most certainly have never seen anyone race to give more than anyone else—all without any scorekeeping or desire for kudos other than the pure joy of seeing others succeed and win. I've also never seen anyone simultaneously solve problems on multiple levels like he does. Tommy's solutions are more than successes for both sides; they're win/win/win…and win.

Some people might think this is because Tommy comes from humble beginnings. Maybe he's overcompensating for being one of the poorest kids in the room, but also one of the smartest kids in the room. Perhaps it's because he's overcome so much adversity with his family dynamics. While all of these experiences have been fuel for his never-quit spirit, Tommy is simply driven by bringing success and joy to others. He believes deeply that, while it's fun to achieve for your own glory, it's 100 times more fun to do it with people succeeding beside and all around you.

Soon after we met, he came to me wanting to hire me as a coach. "I have a lot I'm trying to achieve in the next few months," he said. I immediately knew I should be a mentor to him, not a coach. It was clear to me that Tommy could and would achieve more under his own steam than with the help of a coach. What he really needed was someone in his corner to cheer him on, to talk through disappointments from other people and life, and to give him unconditional support in his desire to help others.

Sometimes my role is to simply reassure him that he's doing well or to tell him he's "pretty," as in adding value and improvement to humanity with his undying efforts. He says that I mentor him but, honestly, he has always given me more than I have given him in time, referrals, and in making sure I know I am also "pretty."

FOREWORD

This book is a treasure that will motivate and inspire you. Enjoy it as a success story in the construction space. Enjoy it as a success story in the LGBTQ+ space. Enjoy it as a rags-to-riches story of hope for every poor, disadvantaged young person alive today.

Tommy's story is only the beginning of what he will achieve. It's just the first chapter of the longer success story of an advocate, friend, mentor, and amazing human being who impacts anyone fortunate to meet him and invests in getting to know him.

Marleta Black
Psychologist, Mentor, and Friend
Bestselling Author of *Say…Something* and *Quinn's Light*

CHAPTER ONE
MY BACKPACK TOLD ME I WAS POOR

"We didn't know we were poor until some smart aleck up and told us." I'm paraphrasing the great Dolly Parton here because if anyone knows about what poverty is really like, it's the woman who repurposed Grandma's shoulder pads as a pushup bra.

When I was growing up in Kathleen, Florida, I didn't know I was poor, either. Everyone around us was in the same boat—living in a double-wide mobile home on a patch of dirt sprinkled with grass, with a bunch of chickens and ducks running around. Until I was in 5th grade, we weren't close enough to civilization to get a pizza delivered, not that we could afford Domino's. Or a computer. Or cable. We were *POOR*, in all capital letters.

To look back and see where I came from and where I am today, all I can say is…wow. To understand the *how* of that journey (and how you can use it to build your own success), though, you need a clear picture of where I started.

The closest gas station was fifteen minutes down the road. Another ten minutes, you'd come across a grocery store, and that was about it. No mall where I could pick up a FUBU T-shirt and pretend I was the Fresh Prince of Bel Air. No Nike sneakers that made me feel like Mike. No vacations to Disney to see the big mouse. My sister and I would play in the weed-choked space that passed for our yard, barefoot and blissfully unaware of how bad it really was.

My parents were only seventeen when my mom got pregnant. They dropped out of high school, got married, and spent most of their lives trying to escape the poverty that sucked them back in when they had me. I think my dad struggled the most with this abrupt change to his plans. I mean, the guy spent five minutes without a condom and missed his prime partying years.

Of course, my dad never let me forget the sacrifice he'd made and how I'd ruined his life. "You should be grateful I put food on the table," he'd say. "You should be grateful I put a roof over your head and let you live here."

I'm pretty sure parents are legally required to feed their children and give them a place to live until they're eighteen. That's part of the deal when you bring the baby home from the hospital. I was, of course, always grateful for the extras (like the rare treat of going out to dinner or a new shirt), but to my dad, food, water, and shelter were luxuries his little party-poopers didn't deserve.

My mom worked at the gas station while my dad worked in construction (I know; I see the irony, too. To be honest, my relationship with my dad was so contentious that I hated everything to do with construction back then). Because they were gone so much, my sister and I spent a lot of time with our grandmother, my mom's mom. Her trailer sat at the other end of that same patch of land, a short walk to a totally different world.

Beside her house, she had tons of gardenia bushes and to this day, the soft, sweet, earthy scent of those white flowers brings me back to those days with my grandma, who was pretty much my best friend when I was little. We'd go to Walmart or Phar-Mor every week to do the grocery shopping, and if we were good, she'd reward us with a rare treat—a Coke Icee or maybe a pack of animal crackers. I still have such a fondness for both that simply seeing them on a store shelf makes me as happy as I was at seven and cracking open a box of Barnum's to chomp the head off a camel.

When *The Lion King* first came out, Grandma took us to the movies, which was akin to going to Disney World for us. We arrived late, after the movie had started, and ended up sitting in one of the front rows. The massive screen loomed over us and Simba looked about thirty feet tall, but we loved every second of the experience, from the chemically buttered popcorn to the cushy seats to the roar of Scar through the speakers.

> My grandma was my rock, the one who bandaged my scraped knees and gave out unconditional hugs.

She was kind and sweet, the quintessential grandmother who thought her grandkids were angels who could do no wrong. I made so many great memories with my grandmother and spent so much time with her that people thought she was my mom (and also because Grandma was in her late thirties when I was little).

I went to school at Kathleen Elementary, which was the same school my mom attended as a young girl. As much as she probably wanted to when she was a kid, she didn't really escape that small-town, poverty-filled life until she was much older. It took her some time to figure out what she wanted to be when she grew up, something I can totally relate to because I was the very definition of late bloomer. But hey, it worked out okay for me, so maybe late bloomers are cooler than people think.

Cool was not how people would have described me when I was in school. I was that nerdy, introverted kid with all the social skills of a three-toed sloth. There were about two dozen kids in my class, but I didn't really make friends with anyone because I had no idea how to navigate the mysteries of small talk or building a launchable tribe. Most of my time at Kathleen Elementary was spent by myself, but I do have two favorite memories from that school: first, my amazing third grade teacher who loved history and had us all dress up in medieval costumes to go to the Renaissance Faire for a field trip, and second, my once-a-week computer lab class.

Kathleen Elementary had a couple of the clunky, boxy Apple IIEs with the green screens (just to put that into perspective—this was around the time Dell released its XPS lineup of desktops with Windows 3.1 while we were clicking away on computers as old as I was). I'd slip in the 5 1/2-inch floppy disk for *Oregon Trail* and become totally immersed in playing the wagon train leader, guiding those hapless pioneers to safety.

I loved *Oregon Trail* partly because the imaginary people in the computer were a lot easier for me to relate to than the other kids in my class, which didn't exactly improve my social standing. I was a lot smarter than most of the people in my grade (in everything except spelling; I'm a terrible speller) and when you're the one who always knows the answer first, that's like hanging a giant *Kick Me* sign on your back. No one likes *that* kid. My teacher tried to explain to me that being smarter was a big reason I didn't fit in, but that wasn't exactly helpful information.

Big surprise that lunch and recess were not my favorite times of day (and don't even get me started on gym class). There were no gifted programs at the school I went to and my parents were so busy keeping the roof over our ungrateful heads that they didn't spend any time nurturing those talents in me. I stuck out like a sore thumb, and as much as I wished I could fit in, there was no pre-determined slot in the Kathleen school system for someone like me.

I only added to my coolness by signing up for FFA—Future Farmers of America—around middle school. I'm sure the other pre-teens working on their deodorant skills were super jealous. I created a mini-farm in the backyard: chickens, ducks, rabbits, pigs, dogs, cats, birds, and even some iguanas. I showed my turkeys at the Florida State Fair and sold them for what I thought was a pretty penny—until I did the math and realized I had spent a lot more money raising them than what the buyer paid me.

Every day it looked more and more like I was going to end up stuck in the same town on the same patch of dirt, working my way through the hundred-year-old middle school and then the ancient local high school, just like my parents had. But then something amazing happened—the state opened a charter school (one of only five at the time) in my school district.

This charter school focused on science and technology. Ooh, unlimited *Oregon Trail* time! By this time, I was as heavily into technology as I could be, all things considered. My grandmother, who worked as a computer operator, saw that interest in me and started bringing home old computers and spare parts from work for me to fiddle with. I'd spend hours taking them apart and putting them back together. I just wanted to know *how do these things work?*

I think it was my mom's idea to enroll me in the charter school and I'm so grateful she did that because it was exactly where I needed to be, academically. When I walked onto that campus, I was stunned because the school was almost like another country. A shiny new weather lab with a satellite link to download the forecast information every day. A computer lab with brand-new computers that had color monitors (and offered a lot more than *Oregon Trail*). Agriculture, construction, medical, and business tracks because the school wanted students to cycle through the different areas of study so they could get a taste of each of those fields. It was literally nerd heaven.

I was part of the inaugural class of sixth graders, all decked out in our matching uniforms and backpacks. I remember being in the carpool line behind shiny, new sedans and SUVs. Our ancient Buick had no working A/C and was rusting away at the seams. The other kids had Trapper Keepers, and I had a stack of bright paper pocket folders from the bargain bin. My sneakers came from Walmart, while the other kids had $100 Nikes (and more than one pair). Even their lunch boxes were nicer than mine.

It was on that first day of school, standing in line waiting to get into the classroom, that I realized I was poor. Virtually every other kid had a thick, heavy backpack with leather trim and sturdy zippered pockets. Mine was a flimsy polyester one my mom bought on sale at Walmart. I remember thinking I wasn't like these other kids who had been to Disney dozens of times. I was never going to own a hundred-dollar pair of sneakers. I lived in a house that sat on cinder blocks, not a concrete foundation.

> My passion for building affordable housing isn't about building a better roof for the adults. It's about giving their kids a shot at living a better life, going to a better school, getting a better night's sleep, and most of all, always feeling safe and warm. And loved.

Around that time, I found a kindred soul named Jennifer, who came from the same type of background I did. We were like two fish out of water in that school. I'd talk to Jennifer every day, but outside of that, I was super shy and self-conscious, which didn't help my social skills at all, even among all the other geeks. I was bullied a little, but not a lot, mainly because this was a school that would kick you out for beating up the nerdy kid after lunch.

Anyone who meets me today would be shocked to hear that I used to be a total introvert who barely spoke in school. The truth is, I didn't get my social groove on until I was in my twenties. In a lot of ways, that was a good thing because it allowed me to watch the world around me and grow some empathy muscles. Plus, it kept me out of trouble, which might have sent me down a totally different path.

Many years later, I remember talking with an employee who was ashamed of where she came from. I realized she was embarrassed to admit she lived in a mobile home. "Do you take care of it?" I asked. She said she did. "Then it's home.

Doesn't matter what type of home it is." I shared with her that I had grown up in a mobile home and that there's always a reason for every set of circumstances. It didn't say anything about her as a person, just like where I grew up didn't say anything about me or dictate my future.

"Never feel bad about where you come from," I advised her that day. "Just keep focusing on where you're going."

When I was a kid, I was always looking past our driveway to see what might be waiting in the world for me. Even if I'd had a crystal ball and a direct dial to the psychic hotline, I never could have predicted the path I'd end up taking.

They say you are what you eat, but just because a person grows up on Hamburger Helper doesn't mean they aren't a grass-fed filet mignon kind of human being.

CHAPTER TWO
THAT TIME I TAUGHT MY MOM ALGEBRA

I think I'm the only person in the world who learned the truth about my conception thanks to Algebra. I was sitting next to my mom, helping her solve a word problem that was ironically close to home: Tommy is 12 years old. The sum of his age and his mother's age is 49. How old was Tommy's mother when he was born?

My mom was having trouble grasping the steps to solve the problem. I thought it might be easier if we tried it with a real-life example, so I plugged in my age, and then added her age at the time. When we solved for X, I realized she was only seventeen when she had me, quite a bit younger than Algebra Mom, who was twenty-five. "Wow. You were only *seventeen?*" I asked.

At the time, I was a teenager in middle school. Seventeen was just around the corner for me. I couldn't imagine being a parent that young. I could barely master color coordination, never mind raising something more complicated than a baby chick.

Sitting there and helping my mom solve algebraic equations was also a really weird role reversal moment. Going back to school was a big deal for my mom, who hadn't even graduated high school (but did get her GED). For years, my mom was a stay-at-home mom but as we got older, she took on a part-time job at the gas station down the street. The job came with zero benefits for her—but the best one for me, a once-a-week treat when she'd bring me home a free scoop of chocolate chip cookie dough ice cream.

My dad didn't make a lot of money, and I think Mom realized that if she wanted to escape the life of poverty she'd been raised in and seemed destined to repeat, she needed to build a career, not just have a job. In the 90s, a woman without a resume pretty much had to have a degree to do that.

The college she chose, Florida Metropolitan University, was a career/technical kind of school, like ITT Tech. My mom didn't ask a lot of questions, didn't do a lot of research, and simply picked the school that was closest to her. Turns out FMU wasn't properly accredited, which made her degree less valuable.

One of her biggest downfalls was her stubbornness about not relying on other people. She was adamant about never asking for help or admitting she didn't understand something.

That came back to bite her with her degree, and later with a life insurance policy she bought that turned out not to cover anything. I think she was afraid of being criticized or looking stupid because she'd been brought up in a pretty critical house. Watching her struggle taught me that it's okay to ask for help and that you don't need to "do it all" yourself. That's a powerful lesson that, sadly, my mother didn't learn until it was too late.

> If you can't do a *Freaky Friday* switch, try putting yourself in the other person's shoes for a bit. The change in perspective can change the relationship.

When she first started taking Algebra—which was a required college course—she got frustrated by the problems and claimed she had a math disability (probably so she didn't have to ask for help). Every night, I'd see her working on her homework at the tiny desk in the corner of my room, muttering about the stupid math problems she couldn't solve.

Math was something I happened to be pretty good at (which came in handy with my FFA turkeys because I'd have to calculate the cost of feed and supplies and then determine the potential profitability [or in my case loss] when selling them. Math also came in handy later, when my husband struggled with Algebra in college, which is another story for another chapter). I was already in Algebra I and was actually a year ahead of all my classmates (I skipped junior year entirely and graduated at sixteen). I offered to help her and could tell it was hard for her to say yes, to admit to her teenaged son that she couldn't do it on her own.

For a couple hours every night, I was the teacher and she was the student. It was a weird hierarchy switch that only lasted until she closed her textbook; then she went back to being a mom and reminding me to brush my teeth.

Helping her was a continual lesson in patience (which, if you've ever met a teenager, is already tough). We'd go through each problem, one at a time, and I'd explain the same steps over and over again. I have no idea where my math and technical skillsets come from, because my mom was not a math person at all.

Sitting beside her at my desk and patiently walking her through solving an equation made me realize that I had reached adulthood—at least intellectually—and how close I was in chronological age to my mom. When you're eleven or twelve, your mom seems old, but when you're thirteen and helping her do algebraic equations you aced a year ago, the age difference becomes really apparent.

College also gave her the opportunity to live out those early twenties moments she had missed because she was raising two kids. I remember one night she got a flat tire and my grandma and I had to go rescue her. My mom was all dressed up and wearing makeup because she'd been at a club with some of the other students. My mom was out clubbing? It was like staring into a time warp.

As my mom made her way through her bachelor's program, and then went on to get her master's degree, I noticed a shift in her. She became more confident and more professional. She was still young, barely over thirty, but determined to carve out a better life. Sometimes my mom's never-take-no approach was embarrassing, because she couldn't take a hint to stop even when it was obvious she should. But her determination is a skill I have adapted, with much more charm and tact (I hope), but nonetheless with the same passion. It's funny how what others saw as my mom's flaws became life lessons for me about strength and perseverance.

When she started studying for her criminal justice degree, she really wanted to be a private investigator, a field she'd been interested in for years. I saw that firsthand when one Christmas, my parents splurged and bought us a Nintendo that came with a game called Déjà Vu. It was one of those spy games where you had to figure out the puzzle in order to get to the next level. My mom dove in, figuring she'd use her powers of deduction to beat the game, but instead the game frustrated her. She was great at reading people emotionally but analytics was not her strong suit.

By the time I was a senior in high school, my parents had temporarily split up and my mom was struggling to make ends meet. She was working as a substitute teacher but that was only part-time, and my dad wasn't working at all. To say it was stressful in our house was an understatement. Even though I was still in high school, I got a job working forty-five hours a week to help out.

"You shouldn't be doing this," she'd say to me as she helped me unload the groceries I'd bought. I think she was pissed that she couldn't afford to feed us and that she had to rely on me to do that. It was Algebra all over again, but it would take a lot longer than a semester to change that situation.

Once she had her degrees, she got a job working for the state Department of Children and Families. Many times, she'd work with families who were struggling in the same state of poverty we had been in for so long, or people who were in much more dire straits and who desperately needed help. It was heartbreaking, difficult work, but her ability to "get" people on an emotional level was a good asset and I think helped her empathize with her clients, many of whom were stuck in situations that would make Rambo cry.

I was the opposite in the emotional maturity department, even after graduating high school. I was still a socially-awkward, introverted nerd who kept on saying all kinds of stupid shit because I had no idea how to fit in as a college freshman (granted, I was only seventeen, so that was probably a big part of the problem). I was too young to get into clubs, so I spent my free time working or going to on-campus events. My inner dorkiness and real age became obvious when I took a girl to a pub on a date. She ordered a beer. "Are you getting one?" she asked.

"No, I'm good," I said, as if it was no big deal.

"Wait...are you even twenty-one yet?"

This was when I had to admit I was only seventeen. Trust me, that's a moment when you stop feeling like a college kid and go right back to being that dorky kid at the front of the room raising your hand because you know all the answers. It was probably just as well that I was too young to drink (and limited my impact on the universe) when I was in college. I would have been a hot mess if I added drinking in with all my other social anxieties.

My mom, however, kept seeing me as a little kid. I wanted to go to school in California and even had a friend who offered me a place to stay, but she said, "Nope. You're not leaving this state," and since I was under eighteen, she could enforce that rule. For a minute, I looked into legal emancipation, but knew that would have created a huge shitshow in my family. I figured I could suck it up until the following June when I would be a legal adult.

Then, a couple months into my freshman year in 2001, September 11th happened. I was living in an off-campus apartment. My mom started blowing up my phone: *You need to leave now. Come home. Bring all your roommates. They can sleep on the floor. Get out of Tampa.* I told her I was just fine and that I didn't want to come home. Her response? *I will call the cops and have them forcefully drag you home.*

> A well-timed joke can be a magic wand in the middle of a tense situation. If you don't have the comedic gene, well...better work on your exit strategies.

I understood that she was worried and on edge, but it wasn't like I was in preschool. I was a college freshman, and perfectly capable of taking care of myself. I bet on the fact that the cops probably had much bigger things to deal with than an almost-adult refusing to follow his mommy's orders, and I did what anyone would have done in that situation to make her stop:

I lied.

The roads are crazy. Tons of people leaving. I'll leave here in a few hours.

I waited until late afternoon, then called her back and said I wasn't coming home. By then, her panic had subsided a little, and although the call was filled with a big lecture, she stopped threatening me with a police escort.

It took her a long time to see me as an adult. Like a *really* long time. When I was eighteen, she took me to the doctor for something and when they called my name, she got up and started walking with me to the room. "Mom, I'm an adult. You don't need to go with me."

"It's my insurance," she said before throwing out the "I'm your mother" card. I argued with her, but she was insistent. The doctor was the one who had to bring down the hammer and tell her that she couldn't come in the room.

My mom, as much as I loved her, was the source of a lot of the problems and tension in our house. Growing up in my house was like living inside a powder keg. Mom was a hair-trigger, lose-her-shit-at-any-moment kind of person and I had to learn at a young age how to defuse a tense situation with a well-timed joke. It didn't take much for an argument between her and my sister to devolve into a shouting match. More than once, I was called home to de-escalate whatever was going on between them.

That did teach me some pretty valuable life skills, though. The construction industry is filled with egos that can be easily bruised. My ability to solve problems, de-escalate conflict, and put my emotions aside has been a huge asset in my career and life. When things seem like they might get out of control, I can step back and assess whether its emotion talking or a true problem.

> In the dick-measuring contest that is the construction industry, there have been times when I've had to remind people who work for me that my pen is bigger. I sign the checks; I'm the boss. When something goes wrong, I don't need to hear their resume—I need them to fix the problem.

That's not to say I never get angry. I simply learned to quickly tame my emotions. I have the same immediate, emotional reactive impulses my mom had, but I've trained myself to wait, analyze, process, and reply. Doing that can take almost any situation and turn it around in a matter of minutes, something that would serve me well when my own life imploded.

Emotional powder kegs are too busy losing their shit to get shit done. Keep that internal TNT under control and you'll be much more successful in life and business.

CHAPTER THREE
I ONLY HAD TO PANIC FOR TWO HOURS

So, about the time I almost sued a national retail store for kicking me out of the loss prevention department...

My first "real" job came when I was sixteen and a well-known big-box store hired me. I started out in the gifts department where I learned more than I needed to know about luggage, how to hang heavy pictures, and the various parts of a lamp (that curved piece of metal on the top of a lamp that connects to the lamp shade is called a harp, by the way. Tuck that little nugget away for the next time the question comes up at Trivia Night).

I did a great job at sales and was promoted pretty quickly to working in the cash room. I was good at math, smart, and responsible, which are pretty crucial job skills when you're working with a lot of money (those turkeys at FFA were a bigger life lesson than anyone thought. I wish I had known about Excel worksheets back then). This was back in the day before debit cards and digital wallets became the way to pay, so we were dealing with stacks of bills on a regular basis.

When I graduated high school, I wanted to transfer from the Lakeland location to a store closer to my college. The security manager who worked with me liked me and told me there was an opening in loss prevention at a store just a few minutes from where I went to school. That job worked out perfectly for me, not just because of the location, but because I enjoyed learning about fraud, being a part of the investigations, and sometimes, actually detaining shoplifters. *Paul Blart, Mall Cop* at his finest. I was only seventeen at the time, but I was good at the job. I even solved a complicated internal theft problem involving an associate at multiple stores. *Columbo*, watch out. There's some competition in the hood.

Then someone told someone else that I wasn't eighteen and that got the attention of the store. Apparently, they felt that minors shouldn't be allowed to work in loss prevention (even though I had graduated high school). They considered it a "hazardous position." Hazardous? It wasn't like I was climbing the power poles or inhaling paint thinner in the stock room.

I checked the law, and the Florida statues contained an exemption for people like me who had worked hard to complete their education early. The store didn't care. They wanted to transfer me to a pricing team. I was not a happy camper, to say the least. I had no desire to roam the store, tagging and counting inventory. Nothing about the situation was fair or right, I told them, but they didn't care. Essentially, I was told to either accept this new position or lose my job entirely.

> Sometimes, life throws you lemons that make pretty lousy lemonade.

My mom had a professor who was an attorney, and when she told her how my employer had broken her son's heart (okay, maybe that's a bit dramatic), she agreed to be my pro bono attorney in the hearing with the unemployment office where I had filed my grievance. I didn't want to take them to court; I simply wanted my job back. In the end, unemployment said the law was the law, and as a minor, I couldn't work in the "hazardous position" of loss prevention. It was just an administrative hearing so I probably could have taken it to court and fought the decision, but it wasn't worth it. Even if I won, the attorney told me, there would be no damages, no compensation. I walked away without a job and with a valuable lesson: what's right doesn't necessarily matter when it comes to the law.

But, the professor/attorney had opened her own practice and offered me a job as her office manager. I spent my college years there, going to events at swanky restaurants with other attorneys, drinking chardonnay and pinot grigio. My college friends were playing beer pong with Natty Ice and learning how to drink from a funnel while I was perfecting my inner sommelier. Being the kid with the glass of Chateau St. Michele at a frat party isn't exactly the key to fitting in (I warned you that I was a nerd—and have a red Solo cup full of pinot to prove it).

I had way more fun dealing with numbers than law, so I ended up leaving the firm for a job at USF as the assistant controller for dining services, working with Aramark. Within a few months, I was bored and wanted more of a challenge so I ended up taking a job with the Longboat Key Club in Sarasota. This was a high-end resort with two golf courses, a spa, two tennis centers, multiple high-end restaurants, beachside condos, and later on, a large marina. Longboat Key Club was a very large, intricate operation.

> The accounting department was headed by a genius of a guy named Bill. I spent three and a half years working for him. Hands-down, he taught me pretty much everything I needed to learn about accounting and just as much about professional development.

By this time, I had gotten married and my wife and I bought a house in Riverview to make the commute a little bit shorter (it was still an hour each way, but better than the hour and a half each way it used to be). I loved my job at Longboat Key Club and was so hungry for knowledge and challenges that they kept promoting me.

Working there was a massive departure from my childhood in a double-wide on a patch of dirt grass, especially given how much money walked through the doors of the Longboat Key Club. Fifteen years ago, the initiation fee just to join the club was $100,000. A person could easily spend a couple thousand dollars a night for a room. We had many high-powered, wealthy guests come to stay, including former presidents. I learned a lot about providing a level of service that was unparalleled and how to solve problems without bothering the client with details.

Watching these people pulling up in Ferraris or spending a winter in a million-dollar condo didn't make me envious—it made me work harder. I watched them move through life with ease and wanted that same peace about paying the bills. Financial security became my goal as I worked my way up in the company and built my career.

Under Bill's tutelage, I became really adept with data analytics and data scrubbing. I also became pretty damned good at Excel and can still whip out a spreadsheet using just key commands (impressive, right?). I spent my days digging deep into the numbers, focusing on helping the operation run as leanly as possible, and learning lessons that have applied to every part of my life and career. Here's the most important thing I learned:

> **If you can job cost a hamburger entree, you can job cost anything.**

The staff at Longboat Key Club became like family to me. They came to my first wedding; they threw me a baby shower (where we played all the silly baby shower games like changing Tootsie Roll filled diapers). It was the type of place where everyone's birthday was celebrated, we decorated for the holidays, and we all brought treats for the office dog, Cash. That, I decided, was how I wanted to run my own business someday.

Driving back and forth to Sarasota, however, wasn't fun. When I was offered the opportunity to head the accounting department at a resort a few minutes from my house, I took it. It was heartbreaking to leave, but I knew I had to keep moving onward and upward to continue my professional development. I still miss the gang at Longboat Key Club, though, and look back at those few years as some of the fondest of my early career.

The new resort was doing well—until the Great Recession of 2009. Overnight, my challenge as director of finance was to not just keep the business afloat, but to find more resources. The business had lent a lot of money to other entities, and bringing that income back into the business made it much more lean, productive, and efficient, which helped them ride out the recession.

Around that time, the owner invested in another business that didn't do that well. The failure of the second business decreased the cash flow in the main business, so they let me go. At the same time, my marriage was falling apart. Around the time our son turned three, my wife and I decided to split up and co-parent our son. Without a doubt, that year was tough for me. So much stress and change hit me all at once, and I had no choice but to find a way through it.

Just when I thought I'd never find another job I loved, I got a call from someone I had met at Longboat Key Club. He worked for a multi-billion-dollar start-up company that was focused on buying single-family homes, fixing them up, and then turning them into rental properties. "You have the aptitude to project manage this," he told me. "I'll teach you whatever you need to know about construction."

Because this venture was so new, neither one of us could predict that we'd soon be dealing with dead bodies, abandoned animals, and hoarder houses that should have been deemed biohazard sites. This wasn't buying the cute three-bedroom at the end of the cul-de-sac and repainting the interior—this was full-on flipping houses that were condemned, abandoned, or foreclosed on…essentially something the company could make money on when they started renting it out.

> I don't care how much Febreze you use, you never get rid of the smell of a dead body in a house. Call that your construction tip for the day: Don't flip the house with the body.

Some of what I saw was heartbreaking. There were houses that people had walked away from, literally in the middle of their lives. There were toys on the living room floor, dishes in the sink, clothes in the closet. Then there were the houses that make great cocktail party stories—filled with boxes of porn or weapons caches; or my favorite, a six-foot pile of disassembled mannequin parts. Maybe it was a new form of a jigsaw puzzle? Whatever it was, I'm not sure I want to know…

The company was busy from Day One. There were months when we flipped *three hundred* houses in thirty days. Ten houses a day is a lot to manage, especially for someone fresh out of college, but I loved the job's challenges.

I also learned a lot about construction. When I started working there, I knew how to paint a wall and change out a toilet, but that was about it. The problems we had to fix ran the gamut from cracked foundations to rodent infestations. There were many times I had to engineer a creative solution that would get the job done on time and on budget. Without even realizing it, I was beginning to disrupt the way the construction industry worked.

Then the company decided to stop acquiring and flipping houses, which meant they didn't need a construction manager anymore, so everyone in my division was let go. They offered me a job in maintenance doing property inspections but then quickly realized I'd be the highest paid inspector in the entire company. Almost as soon as they offered me the job, they called me back and said, "Never mind. We're not going to keep you on. Oh, and can you bring back the company car today?"

In an instant, I was jobless and carless. I didn't have my contractor's license yet so I couldn't become a contractor, which meant I probably couldn't stay in the field I'd grown quite skilled at. On top of that, I had just signed a contract on a rental house that was more expensive than where I'd been living before. I had a son to support. Bills to pay. A car to buy.

What the hell was I going to do?

Two hours later, I got a call from a construction company who had done work for the company that let me go. They offered me a job, but I had misgivings about their business practices. I didn't want to get locked into a contract and a non-compete with a company I didn't trust, so I turned down the job.

I was still jobless and carless, but I was also pretty resilient and maybe a little cocky because that job offer told me other people valued my skills. I mean, if I'd saved other companies hundreds of thousands of dollars and run a pretty tight flipping ship, why couldn't I do that for myself? At the time, flipping to rent was a newly formed subset of the construction industry, and only a handful of people nationwide had this type of experience. People like me. That's when a lightbulb went off in my brain. Actually, it was maybe more like a SpaceX rocket lighting up my mental sky.

I had a colleague with a contractor's license who hadn't pulled the trigger on going into business for himself. I called him up and said, "Let's start a business doing the same thing the other company was doing. We'll go fifty/fifty and work our asses off." He said yes, we went into business, and I started networking like a maniac trying to build our sales.

One thing about networking—you never know when a connection will become a game-changer. I had connected with someone on LinkedIn who was the vice president for a property investment company which happened to be a competitor of the company that let me go. I sent him a cold-call email—a risk that resulted in a million dollars in sales for our new little company. When I met with him in person, he told me why he was impressed with me. "In that one email, you identified my problem and told me exactly how you would solve it." That meeting for one house turned into thirty houses a month.

Now we had a new kind of thing to panic about—turnaround times. But we figured it out when the checks started coming in and the work started filling our calendars. I remember seeing the first big check (which isn't big by construction budget standards) for $30,000 and realizing, *Hey, maybe I can do this.*

And of course, that was the moment when everything changed. Again.

Taking the leap into working for yourself will undoubtedly be the most terrifying thing you ever do—and quite possibly the most rewarding.

CHAPTER FOUR
MY FAKE SELF SHOWED UP FOR WORK TODAY

I know you're dying to ask. In fact, you might have just read a couple sentences twice and wondered if there was a typo.

There wasn't. It's called real life—my real life.

Even though this part of my story really isn't anyone's business, I can appreciate the curiosity.

> After all, if we can't be genuine about who we are and how we got here, what are we doing?

Yes, I married a woman the first time around, and yes, I am now very happily married to a great person who happens to be a man.

That marriage, by the way, almost didn't happen. When he walked off the elevator an hour late (and I was an hour early, so I'd waited two hours total) *and* wearing red shorts to a fancy rooftop bar on our first date, I probably should have bailed. Instead, I stayed. And that date with Nathan changed my life in ways I never saw coming.

Let me back up a bit. At the time I met my husband, I was in a period of living a delayed frat life. I'd had a college bromance but not really done much of the typical college experience. All those things I put off while graduating early and then getting married and having a kid became my new single life once I got divorced. I'd hit karaoke bars with friends or take off on impromptu Key West party trips with a bunch of female friends. Side note: did you know you can order a bucket of beer at 8am? Thank you Denny's Key West! But while I was doing all these things, I was hiding my real self from the people closest to me.

I dated both men and women but kept my dates with men a secret. Partly because I was still figuring out who I was and what I wanted, whether I was bi or gay, and how the hell I was going to work in a manly field like construction if people found out I was dating guys. I thought there was no one else like me in construction.

Those weekend trips were a blast because I could easily sneak off and hit a gay bar while the girls were doing their thing. When I was closer to home, I lived in constant fear that someone I knew would see me with a guy. I remember being at a gay resort in St. Pete during Pride month. I was in the pool when I saw a vendor of ours walk up. We made eye contact and I panicked.

I couldn't run away—for one, I was standing in the middle of the pool, and for another, he had already seen me. I waited for him to say something, call me out, criticize me, something. Instead, he said, "Hi," and I said "Hi" back, and that was it.

It was the first time I realized that other people in the LGBTQ+ community very rarely out each other. We know how big of a decision that is and that, in some places, being out can have serious career and life ramifications.

Still, I worried every time I logged into a dating app (under any of my alternate-named profiles) that someone would see me or say something. I stressed that coming out would make me lose a contract or a client. Gay marriage wasn't legal back then, and there were still many people who couldn't accept or understand any other lifestyle than their own. Plus, did I mention I worked in the *construction* industry?

I dated a lot of people once or twice, never really getting attached or being public about what I was doing. I'd bail at the pinkest hint of a red flag.

Then I met Nathan. That first August night, we talked for hours, sitting in the rooftop bar at the Birchwood Canopy in St. Pete. We went from there to another bar, and another, singing karaoke, walking in the park, and exchanging our first kiss. For our second date, he offered to cook me dinner.

It very quickly became something serious. We were at different places in our lives—I was thirty and building a company and he was twenty-three and still working to afford his own home—but something between us clicked and felt right. By September, we were an official couple but not out in public yet. When people asked me what I did over the weekend, I'd lie and say I stayed home or went to the movies with my "friends" instead of telling the truth—I was with my boyfriend and we had a great time.

Then came Halloween.

You should know that I love Halloween—like *really* love Halloween—and have ever since my mom hosted a Halloween party for me and the kids from my school when I was in first or second grade. We played games, she handed out treat bags, and I became hooked forever on pumpkins and ghosts and reasons to throw a kickass event. For several years in a row now, I raid Spirit's inventory of spooky décor and throw a rocking Halloween party.

That year, Nathan had been debating going back into competitive color guard where he had already achieved an international gold medal. If he kept competing, it would mean he'd be traveling all fall and winter. When he decided to stay in town and go back to college instead, I realized I now had a date for my Halloween party. A date I really wanted my friends to finally get to know.

> I tried a new thing that day—honesty. I was absolutely terrified, but it turns out honesty is a pretty freeing policy.

I knew what that meant—being honest. I called up my best friend Gary the morning of the party. "I, uh, have someone coming to my party as my date," I said.

"Okay," he replied, clearly wondering why I was announcing that.

"And that person's a guy," I said.

The phone went dead silent.

I was terrified of what that silence meant. Then, after a minute, my friend went back to talking about ordinary things, as if this was any old call. Just before we hung up, I worked up the courage to ask him if he was okay with me dating a guy.

"Tommy," he said, "a while ago you asked me how I would feel if my son came out as gay and whether I'd still love him." He paused for a moment before he continued. "The answer is yes. Yes I would still love him the same." It was one of the most impactful things anyone has said to me in my life.

That told me all I needed to know about my friends. Every one of them accepted Nathan and our relationship just like they would any relationship. It gave me a sense of ease and relief to be able to talk to them about this great guy I was falling for, or to proudly show up at an event with Nathan on my arm. When Thanksgiving rolled around, I called my mom and told her about Nathan. She was totally cool with it.

Then I called my grandma. She's a fantastic grandma, but she's also an old Southern woman with a few old Southern woman biases. I told her I was dating a gay Black man. She started to cry. Then I cried. It was, to put it mildly, a rough conversation.

"Well," she finally said, "I'll be nice to him. But I'm not going to like it." It took her some time, but she was very excited to be part of the processional when our wedding day came. Fast forward a couple of years and they're now best friends who go to KFC and Big Lots together.

The biggest test came with my career. Let's face it—if I was living in New York City and came out as a gay man, it would be no big deal. Tampa is pretty open, but not every part of this state is so understanding about what other people see as "alternate" lifestyles. There's still plenty of housing and job discrimination, even if people don't say out loud that they turned down the application because it was two men applying to live in a one-bedroom apartment.

That fear of judgment or retaliation had been in my head for a long time. I remember reading about the horrific murder of twenty-one-year-old Matthew Shepard in 1998, who was tortured and killed just because he was gay. At the time, I was around his age, and I was shocked that kids could hate other kids that much. I had seen friends get their asses kicked for showing any kind of sign of being effeminate and was terrified that could be me.

When I met Nathan, I didn't want to be afraid anymore and I didn't want to lie one more time about how I'd spent my weekend. I didn't make a big announcement or anything. I just subtly (and sometimes not so subtly) let people know I was dating a man.

One of the more memorable ways I did that was at a networking event, which was filled with guys in power suits. I was standing with a group of guys when a really pretty woman walked by. A couple of them said, "Wow. That is an attractive girl." They turned to me, waiting for me to agree with their manly view of a woman.

"Yes, she's attractive," I said, "but my husband said no more girls."

The joke took a second to sink in. As it did, I saw this huge look of fear in the eyes of the other guys. I could tell they were thinking, *Did I just screw up and offend the gay guy?*

Then I laughed and they laughed and life went back to normal. We talked about our families, complained about our spouses, and found common ground in being family-oriented men. Here's a secret: gay people and straight people have the same arguments over what's for dinner and where to go on vacation.

> In business, it's more valuable to be genuine than un-genuine. The old adage about working with people you know, like, and trust, is true. When you are the person you say you are, people get to know you, like you, and—most of all—trust you.

A lot of people think I'm straight when they meet me, so they're surprised when I mention my husband. "Don't take this the wrong way," they'll say, "but until you mentioned a husband, I had no idea you were gay." I tell them that's okay because I had no idea they were straight… Because I don't ask, and I don't care.

Today, I'm proud of who I am, as I am. I have a diversity certification for my business (and am one of only fifty certified LGBT-Business Enterprises in the construction industry nationwide). If someone throws slurs at someone else in our workplace, we're done with them. I don't want anyone who works for me—no matter their gender, race, or sexuality—to feel unsafe when they come to work.

Instead of hiding who I am, I'm trying to be a leader who paves the way for the Matthew Shepards of the world to feel safe and to be embraced, not murdered. If I can stop one person from being hurt or from taking their own life, that will be worth every moment of hesitation and fear I felt.

Here's the golden rule I wish everyone followed: It's okay to be uncomfortable with something you don't know or understand. Just don't be uncool or cruel, or see that person as anything other than a person.

> If you can't be true to yourself, you can't be true to anyone, or anything, else.

CHAPTER FIVE
DON'T TAKE ADVICE FROM PEOPLE GOING THE WRONG DIRECTION

In the days before GPS, paper roadmaps were the only way to know where you were going. If you didn't have a map, you'd have to stop at a roadside gas station and ask some guy in greasy coveralls how to get where you were going. "Take a right at the big tree and go down the road by the green mailbox with the weird numbers. Can't miss it." Frankly, with those kinds of directions, you'd be more likely to end up five states away than where you wanted to be.

It's pretty much the same thing when you go into business for yourself. There's no roadmap, no GPS telling you what to do, and a lot of people give you advice that is about as helpful as an extra tail on a cat.

At least once a week after I started that business, I was terrified I'd made the wrong decision. The bigger the money got, the higher the stakes, and the more a mistake would cost me. When you go a thousand dollars over budget on a reno, it's not as company-crushing as going a hundred thousand dollars over. I learned to figure out solutions to whatever arose pretty quickly, and to be humble enough to ask advice from people with more experience when I had no idea how to solve the problem.

There were plenty of seasoned people who looked down on me because I was a good fifteen to twenty years younger and had a fraction of their experience. Sometimes, they saw me as competition and they'd pull out the "I know more than you do" attitude to try to prove their point. Or worse, the "when you're older, you'll understand this."

Instead of resenting them, I respected their experience and knowledge because many of the people I worked with definitely knew their stuff. In fact, I've met plenty of people in this industry who knew as much—or more—than a general contractor but had never gotten their own GC license, either because they didn't want to, they had test anxiety, or they couldn't afford the schooling. I took the test and can definitely attest to how many small details you need to know in order to pass, random things like the exact thickness of rebar used in different concrete pours.

Having my license did help make the owners and other contractors we worked with take me more seriously. They realized I was as committed as they were to this business, and that I was there to work *with* them, not order them around.

> Coming off as a know-it-all only antagonizes people and disrespects their experience. If I disagree with the process a subcontractor wants to use, I don't disrespect them. Instead, I ask them to explain the why behind their choice.

Ninety-nine percent of the time, I have found that math speaks louder than anything else when it comes to making the best decision for the job and the company. In a heated discussion about the best way to do something, I'll hear the other person out, take notes about their recommendation, and then do the math. Sometimes, their option made the most cost-efficient sense, sometimes mine did. Either way, once you bring data to the table, it validates your point.

I know I can't do my job without these professionals, and just because I write the checks doesn't make me more valuable. If they need a vacation or to stay home with a sick kid, I want to know and make that work for them. They're the backbone of everything we do.

Unlike a lot of industries, in construction, you run into the same handful of problems again and again on every job site. Most of the time, solving that problem is about working backwards from the deadline to the starting point. I'll start by asking: *What's your goal?*

If the answer is, for example: *To get the walls painted before the end of next week.*

Then I work backwards on the how to attain that goal. Painting before the end of next week means several other things have to happen first depending on where we are in the job process. Before we paint, we need to do the texture, but before that, we need to hang the drywall, and before that, we have to repair the plumbing and electrical. If the plumbing and electrical are fixed by Thursday, we can hang drywall Friday and be painting by the following Tuesday and be done with that by Friday morning. Boom. Problem solved.

The difference with working for a company and being the company owner is the level of responsibility. I didn't have a fairy godmother to fix everything going wrong and drop a check on my desk after she did it, which meant I had to learn how to fix every single problem that arose, whether that was something in my wheelhouse or not.

I had a massive wakeup call when I realized that every decision I made wasn't going to affect just my family—but the families of every person who worked for me and the families of every house we renovated. At the very least, if we screwed up, we could lose money and not be able to meet payroll. If we *really* screwed up, someone would end up living in an unsafe house that could harm them or their kids, and open us up to a company-ending lawsuit.

Thinking about all those what ifs and consequences made stress my constant companion. Like a dog that pees on the carpet, eats the toilet paper, tracks mud across your white carpet, and then barks incessantly.

Only worse.

I remember the first time I had to let someone go and how difficult it was to make that decision, even though I knew it was the right thing. Some people handle firing an employee by just getting really pissed off at the person they're letting go. I can't do that. I try to empathize and be compassionate when I let someone go or sever a relationship with a subcontractor.

Despite my best efforts to not make it an unpleasant experience, doing that ruins my entire day. I know that I am changing their lives when I do that, but the flip side of that means I can change someone else's life by bringing them onto my payroll. Hiring the right person for the right position can also change the entire company—and make everyone's lives better.

There were a few days (maybe more than a few) when I thought about going back to the regular workforce. I could take all my skills and easily earn six figures on someone else's payroll. Let them have the headaches and the heartburn. Trust me, some days it was really, really tempting, especially as I was still trying to figure out this entrepreneur thing.

There's an old saying that you "fake it till you make it." I hate that saying because it implies you're not using the skills you have. Yes, I had to act a lot more confident than I felt when I first started out, but I never faked my abilities. If I didn't know something, I asked. If I had a great solution to a problem, I spoke up.

The trick is knowing whether that solution is the right one for *you*. When we started the first company (back when I was still pretty green in this industry), another contractor gave me some advice that just didn't ring true. Their suggestions seemed a lot like bid rigging. People go to jail for that kind of thing. I trusted my instincts and ignored that advice. Probably a really good thing because I don't look very good in stripes.

There is a certain degree of pressure on an owner to look like you have it all together, even if you don't. If I go into a project sweating bullets and stressing about the finances, it's not going to give the crew a good feeling. That ripple effect can roll through a company in seconds. So, I kept the majority of those fears from the crew if I was worried about something going wrong.

> There are also times when you just have to admit to others that this shit is scary and you're trying to figure it out.

In the end, the simple truth is I love what I do. I've learned a lot over the years, soaking up the knowledge the experienced subcontractors have, while never being afraid to shake things up once in a while. Necessity is, after all, the mother of invention—and when you have a renovation project that has gone completely sideways, sometimes you have to get inventive to find a safe, cost-effective, working solution.

That's the challenge that gets me out of bed every day. I get to move around, wear different hats, and focus on a variety of things. One area jogs another area of my brain; and no matter how tough the problem, there's always a solution.

Here's the truth I learned early on: all those people who were older—the ones I thought had it all together and who never sweated a payroll—they were faking it some of the time, too. None of us has a secret roadmap or all of the answers (or a fairy godmother). We're all just doing the best we can to keep moving forward.

And don't forget that left turn by the green mailbox with the upside-down numbers. It'll get you right where you want to be. Sort of.

You don't have to know exactly where you're going to take the first step.

CHAPTER SIX
I'M NOT YOUR INTERIOR DESIGNER

Let's get this out of the way, before you drag me into Sherwin-Williams and start asking me whether I think you should paint your kitchen Glimmer or Sea Salt. I'm not your interior decorator. I'm not a color gay or a fashion gay (if you've seen me in real life, that's pretty evident). I'm so far away from the image of the stereotypical gay man that the other gays have threatened to revoke my gay card.

Not really. Well, maybe.

I have never fit a stereotype of anything and I'm pretty proud of that. I don't want to be a carbon copy of others—not in the way I act, dress, or the way I run my business. If I can't expand the definition of what a gay man is or what a contractor brings to the table, then what am I doing here?

The stereotypical contractor yells a lot, stomps off the job when people don't do what's expected of them, and sits back in his creaky office chair to enjoy an end-of-the-day cigar. I'm not that guy. I'm the one who comes at a problem from the perspective of working with people to figure out a solution, not screaming at them like I'm Gordon Ramsey. I like to use math, not f-bombs.

One of our renovation jobs had a problem with the skim coat on the drywall not drying. Day one goes by, it's damp. Day two goes by, it's still damp. This put the job behind and cost us money. When day three came and the drywall was still damp, the subcontractor finally told me about it.

I realized it was super humid out, and that part of the house didn't have any A/C in it because it was sealed off (you can't pump in air that has nowhere to go). I went to Home Depot, rented a dehumidifier for fifty bucks, plugged it in, and the drywall was ready for sanding and a finish coat a few hours later. I'd solved a problem that cost us far more than that simple fix.

"Next time, please tell me about a problem like this on day one. We could have spent $50 and saved two days," I said to the subcontractor. I think he was scared I'd get angry, but when I didn't toss a table or throw a frying pan at his head, he felt more comfortable coming to me with problems.

> **If you can hold off freaking out, you'll find it's a lot easier to solve problems. Plus, your staff isn't scared of you—always a good thing.**

Another non-stereotypical boss thing: I'd rather overly communicate with people than let problems fester. I want people to feel safe to come to me and admit when they don't know something (I'll readily tell people when I don't know something because I'd rather learn from the experienced masters in that field than bumble along and make a mistake). Instead of doing the Big Boss Freakout, I try to empower the people who work with me to tackle a problem that's new to them. I love it when one of my employees says, "I haven't tried this before but I can figure it out. I want to give it a shot."

Dealing with my mom taught me to be calm in an "emergency." My mother was the kind of person who made her emergencies into everyone else's problem to solve. She'd get ramped up over the smallest issue and expect me or my sister to drop everything and help her fix it. That tendency got worse in the last two years of her life. Instead of telling her no, I took a deep breath and helped her.

Here's a valuable life tip for you: When someone's dying, it's not really the time to enforce boundaries. Just let that shit go.

Sometimes, people just need to vent their fears. A renovation can be a scary prospect for a client. They're spending a lot of money, trusting you with their most valuable possession, and praying it turns out right. That means the contractor really needs to listen, yet also be the voice of reason.

Clients know I'm not the contractor who proposes an expensive reno that only makes my bottom line look good. I've been in the boat of scrimping and saving for a new kitchen and I get that this is a huge decision for them. I don't want any of my clients to buy into market stereotypes and fast fads without really thinking through their decisions.

Before we even start a renovation, I ask the client where they stand in terms of selling the house. If they are planning on selling it within a year, that makes a difference in terms of where I'd advise they put their money (kitchens and bathrooms, hands-down, are worth the investment).

If I know the client has no intention of staying in the house forever, I will talk them out of big-concept, costly structural changes because they won't recoup those costs in the sale. I don't disagree that opening up the living room and kitchen will look fantastic, but I want them to know doing that will end up costing more than its worth. When it comes to where you lay your head at night, sometimes there are far more important things than profits.

I'm also having those conversations with the people who believe they have a "brand" look to the houses they flip. Reality check needed here. *The average consumer has no idea and probably doesn't care if you have a brand look.* They want to buy the house that is right for their lives, right for their budget, and right for the area. If you spend an extra $50,000 creating an open concept with blue hues on the walls because that's your brand, you've probably just created the most expensive open-concept blue houses in several neighborhoods. Inevitably, your commitment to your "brand" is going to make the houses sit on the market longer.

Most of us know you have to take personal attachment out of the equation when you're intending to flip. You can't paint the walls purple because it's your favorite color. You have to paint them a neutral color so that non-purple loving people can picture themselves living there (I don't have to be an interior decorator to know that). But hey, if you're really committed to purple, add a few purple pillows to the tan sofa.

You also don't want to go too far in the neutral direction. There's a balance to hit when it comes to resale value, and you have to decide which you value more—how quickly that sale gets into your bank account or how committed you are to those octopi tiles in the bathroom.

> Do the math, then decide what matters most to you.

On the flip side are the people who live in a house that's caught in a constant state of suspended animation. "Someday" they're going to sell the house. That day could be two years or ten years from now. In the meantime, don't you want to live in a house you love?

I worked with a client who wanted to expand their primary bedroom. Doing so would mean turning one of the guest bedrooms into primary bedroom space. Yes, they'd have a huge walk-in closet and amazing bathroom, but they worried that doing that would hurt the resale value.

"How long do you plan to live in this house?" I asked them.

"Until the day we die," said the homeowner.

"Then live in a place that makes you happy. Besides," I said, "the kids will probably level the house and build a new one when you're gone anyway." That made the couple laugh. Ultimately, they did what made them happy, and that gave them an amazing closet in the much-bigger primary bedroom.

If you're not sure and you're in the "maybe we'll sell" category, you can always take a moderate approach. You can change out a light fixture when you put it on the market, but it's a lot harder to reinstall a wall you tore out. It's easy to switch to a more modern faucet, but it'll cost you big bucks to change that bright-colored granite. Know your numbers and decide what matters most to you.

Here's the truth: You don't have to fit a stereotype any more than I do. Don't worry whether your house looks like the Smiths. Chances are the Smiths hate those taupe walls and white countertops anyway.

Your home is your safe space. It's the place that welcomes you after a bad day and a horrible traffic jam. Be a little vulnerable in decorating it and make it your own (just don't ask me for help).

I've been reading *Dare to Lead* by Brene Brown, a book I recommend everyone read. In the book, she tells a story about speaking in front of a group of military brass. "Can anybody in this office, or anybody in this presentation, say that they have had a significant challenge without confronting vulnerability?" No one raised their hand. Finally, one guy stood up and said, "I've done three tours. I've been in multiple combat situations. And there's no challenge I have overcome without having to expose myself to vulnerability."

I love that story because it proves that vulnerability is not a weakness. Vulnerability is just identifying what you are afraid of so you can get past it and feel safe. That's what home is to me, the place that makes you feel safe. That's why it doesn't make sense to decorate it with hostile colors that make you uncomfortable or annoyed.

That's as true for adults as it is for children. Children can't get a good night's sleep if they don't feel safe in their house and comfortable in their space.

The house I grew up in wasn't perfect or super safe (especially in a hurricane), but it was a safe spot for me. I had all these little touches in my room that personalized my space: Lego creations, comic strips I'd torn out of the paper, Star Trek ship models, basically all the normal nerdy kid stuff. I had lots of great memories there that all vanished when my parents took the house apart.

With double-wide manufactured homes like that, the house is built in two pieces and put together on site. Ours was an older home, built in the 80s, and it had a lot of problems. When those problems became too costly to fix, they decided to replace the entire thing. I watched my old home leave the driveway on the back of a semi, which was oddly disconcerting. Most people never see their house driven away to the dump.

I went into my "new" room, which now sported an oversized chair and looked like a little living room. The comic book strips I'd taped on the walls were gone, and there weren't any Legos lurking in the carpet waiting to be stepped on. It was so weird to be in this new space that felt nothing like the old one. Even though my address hadn't changed, it didn't feel like home and didn't feel safe; and it never really did again.

At least not until I found my own house with Nathan and we decorated it with the little touches that feel as welcoming as my childhood bedroom did. That's what I want when I walk in the house at the end of the day—to feel like I've finally arrived where I need to be.

I can still remember the day they brought grandma's trailer and set it up on our little patch of land. I was only four or five, but I remember she closed on my birthday and had her trailer set near our lone little peach tree. I have a memory of putting pennies into an outlet and the outlet sparking. Don't try that at home, kids, no matter how inquisitive you are.

My childhood bedroom and my adult-life house aren't going to be in *Architectural Digest* anytime soon, but that's okay.

Those spaces suit who I am, who I want to be, and what I want to come home to. That means you're going to see a painting of a six-fingered Grinch at Christmas and a set of high school lockers in the dining room instead of a buffet. Those things make me happy, which really is the only thing I care about when it comes to decorating.

Freaking out when a problem arises only puts your brain further away from finding the solution.

CHAPTER SEVEN
THE CHANGE ORDERS CAN KILL YOU

I think that HGTV should come with a trigger warning for shows like Love it or List it or 100 Day Dream Home because, frankly, that shit is not at all realistic. More than once, I've caught a snippet of one of those shows in a waiting room and it's been all I can do not to start screaming at the TV like a guy who played five minutes of football in high school who's screaming at the Bucs.

In the real world of building permits and transit delays, not to mention problems lurking under the floors and behind the drywall, things can definitely go wrong. Projects can get delayed. And then honest, tough conversations need to be had.

Then there's the flip side of people who expect their reno to be like the movie *Money Pit,* where Tom Hanks's character,

Walter, asks the contractor how long it will take them to do some (pretty extensive) renovations. "Two weeks," Curly, the contractor says.

"Two weeks? That's amazing," Walter replies.

Under his breath, Curly says, "Amazing nothing. It'll be a regular miracle."

What follows is a disaster of epic proportions that takes about a hundred times longer than two weeks to fix. In my line of work, I've heard more HGTV and *Money Pit* jokes than I can count because there are still a lot of people out there who think we can pull off a full kitchen reno in an hour, just like on TV. Those are the type of people who end up calling me back a few months later after their one-hour special contractor left them with hanging wires and dysfunctional plumbing.

I get that people are impatient. When you're renovating one of the main arteries of the house, it can seem like an eternity of eating takeout on paper plates. The stress factor can be huge. Homeowners want the job done, and they want it done *now*. Things simply don't work that way, and a lot of people figure that out when they attempt a DIY reno.

> Hate to break it to you, but HGTV is not real life. Flipping a house that fast only happens on a TV or movie screen.

We're the generation that has lost the ability to sew a scarf, but get a few hours of YouTube under our belts and everybody suddenly thinks they're Bob Vila. Then you open up the walls and find things you aren't prepared for (or skilled enough to deal with) and you quickly realize there's a lot more to renovation work than just watching a video and making a Home Depot run.

Sometimes, we're just as surprised as the homeowner to find an electrical rat's nest (or even a real rat's nest) in the walls. The best thing to do, I've found, is to tell the homeowner the truth and explain the why behind the delay. "It's not going to be a two-week job. It's realistically going to take two months or longer." When we find leaky plumbing in the walls or knob-and-tube wiring stuffed into the insulation, we tell the client right away. I try to lead with empathy and understanding because I know how much people love their homes and how difficult it is to be without them. It never fails though; someone will get angry at me about the conditions of their home when we're in the middle of a renovation. I think it's startling to see the walls opened up or the flooring removed, so it's understandable. I sometimes find myself playing their counselor, allowing people to vent their frustrations so we can move along.

Reality TV, as we all know, is not at all real. I've talked to producers about the behind-the-scenes environment of a "reality" show and know that it takes tens of hours of footage to get a usable hour for TV. That's what's happening on a job site, many times over. There are dozens and dozens of hours of tedious work, dozens and dozens of changes and microproblems we've had to deal with, and dozens of conversations with the homeowner about changes they may or may not need to make, all before we get to the big reveal.

Then there's the government. City and town governments don't have fully-staffed customer service departments for one simple reason—they don't care about making your customer experience better. You can't just choose another city like you can a cable provider. You're pretty much stuck with those government offices until you move. We've had nightmares with inspectors not showing up on time or taking weeks to get back to us, all of which put a job seriously behind.

Let's not forget the inspector who did, in his own way, show up—and proceed to write us up for not having the right changes on a two-story house that we weren't working on. In fact, we were remodeling a one-story *ranch*. It took months for us to finally show him that we weren't even working on a two-story house and that he had his addresses confused (or maybe he was a little height-challenged, I'm not sure).

When you factor in a bunch of change orders ("Can you add three feet of cabinets? What if we change out the flooring? Can we remove that wall you just built?"), the process can drag on even longer. I hear those requests all the time, but my personal favorite is: "We know we told you to paint the walls this color, but we don't like it after all. Can you repaint it for free?" Yes, this actually happened to me on a job (a few of them, honestly).

Change takes time. It's almost always filled with a lot of backsteps and rewrites. Moments you regret and moments that change everything. As I began to grow into my life as an entrepreneur, I went through a lot of changes in my personal and professional life. There were a lot of scary moments and a lot of wonderful ones.

Okay, so maybe there were a lot more scary moments than wonderful, especially early on. I wanted to be an overnight success (hey, who doesn't) and there were days when I was frustrated that it was taking too long to get there. Taylor Swift, after all, made it in her twenties, but Oprah made it in her forties and her success has been just as big (if not bigger). Who are we kidding, Oprah's is definitely way bigger!

There were moments when I doubted the process and moments when I was a little scared about making the rent. Like a renovation, there were plenty of curveballs that came out of left field. My husband has taken it all in stride, which I think made it much easier for me to do the same.

He has a way of breaking down the problem and making it simpler. If I get off track and start projecting too far into the future, he'll say, "Stop. Let's focus on this and focus only on today. What are we doing today?" Because, in the end, that's really all you can do. No matter how hard you try, you can't predict everything that's going to happen tomorrow or over the next two weeks. You can't foresee how this change will affect that one, or how what initially seemed like a simple virus can cripple an entire industry.

Or an entire business. Like mine.

> Most "overnight" success stories are decades of blood, sweat, and tears. If you're not where you want to be today, then maybe you gotta sweat it out a little longer.

CHAPTER EIGHT
KNOW WHAT YOUR LUNCH IS WORTH

I've always admired Henry Ford. Yes, that Ford, the one who invented the automobile; not just because of his entrepreneurial success, but for how spectacularly he failed. And failed. And failed. It took decades for him to get it right and to create the Ford Motor Company that would later change the world.

Way before the Model T, Ford started with the Quadricycle, his first version of an automobile, and he was laughed out of every investor meeting. He eventually found a business partner who helped him start the Detroit Automotive Company, but within a year and a half, that company was dissolved and Ford was left without a job (or a car he could sell to consumers). He tried again, even convincing his original business partner to back him a second time, but when Ford didn't produce a sellable automobile fast enough, the business partner replaced Ford at the helm of his own company. That had to be pretty damned demoralizing.

Ford didn't let that keep him down for long. He went back to the drawing board, redesigning the Model T to better fit the needs of consumers, and to also make it cheaper and faster to build. He came back to Ford Motor Company, got the Model T into production, and became an overnight success. When demand outpaced supply, he invented a mass production model that got cars off the assembly line quicker. He adapted and changed as needed until he found the right method for his particular madness.

There are dozens of lessons for entrepreneurs in Ford's story. Things I've experienced myself—business partnerships that fell apart, products that needed to be changed to fit the market, and an overwhelming demand that meant reconfiguring to keep up with the work. And failure, plenty of failure.

I also dealt with one thing that Henry Ford never had to—a worldwide pandemic that shut down businesses across the globe, and left me, a brand-new solopreneur, with absolutely zero business to build.

Before I get to the havoc Covid wreaked on my business (and how I climbed out of that mess), I want to talk about worth because I think that's what really got me through the pandemic and brought me to where I am today. If I hadn't learned some lessons about self-worth before Covid, I probably wouldn't have been able to get back on my feet entrepreneurially, because so much of being successful inside yourself is, in my opinion, about how you define worth.

Failure is a part of life. I know because I've failed more times than I can count and am pretty vocal about those flops when I talk to other business owners. I failed early on in my journey and, like Ford, I failed spectacularly.

> I had a choice—I could wallow in the misery of failure, or I could pick myself up and try again. That meant admitting to others I had failed and that I was struggling to get back to where I was.

It was tough because, at the time, I thought I'd be at a certain level before I was in my thirties and I was so ready to be the success story I'd been working toward for so long. Just when that started to happen, Covid pulled the rug out from under me.

Most people are afraid to talk about how many times they've fallen on their butts. They feel like someone else is going to judge them for failing.

Truthfully, people *are* going to judge you for failing. And when they do, they've done you a favor. That's when you know those people are not your people. Most of the people doing all the judging and behind-your-back whispering have never had real success themselves. It's like the story of the crabs in the bucket—one crab tries to get out and all the other crabs start pulling him back. They're so invested in keeping him down there with them that they don't even realize they are pinning down the one crab smart enough to escape before Chef Ramsey throws them all into a casserole.

Don't be those crabs. Be the one who climbs out of the bucket.

The most successful people have fallen—and fallen hard—at least once before they got to the top. They didn't let what other people thought about their failures stop them. They didn't take it personally. They ignored those judgmental comments and just went right back to scaling the bucket.

> The crabs who pin each other down to get to the top aren't your people because they're just shell-fish. Ba-dum-dum.

I've always been driven but I haven't always embraced my own uniqueness. It wasn't until I decided "this is who I am and who I'm going to be" that I realized I was happier and more successful in all areas of my life. It wasn't easy at first to talk about having a husband at a construction convention or to put a rainbow on my hard hat. It took me a minute to stop caring what other people thought and to just be myself. Today, I am absolutely unapologetically me, whether I'm at home or talking with an investor.

In a meeting today, someone said to me, "I've been watching you and I can tell you're not like the average person."

I took that as one of the best compliments I've had in a while and great proof that being myself is making me grow more than I ever thought possible. The minute I start going back to trying to be like all the other crabs is the minute I stop using what makes me uniquely *me* and then make less of a difference in the world.

Don't worry; this chapter isn't about to become a whole Kumbaya, let's-sit-around-the-campfire-and-hug kind of moment. I do think, though, that it's important to talk about the concept of worth and how that ties in with success. Men tend to equate the trappings of success—like owning a different Rolex for every day of the week—with what they are worth. If they're not keeping up with Mr. Jones down the street who just bought a Lambo, they aren't worth much in the job market or in the world (or to others).

So, they keep wearing Armani suits and pretending everything is perfect when, in fact, they might be mortgaged to the hilt and worried that the repo guy is coming for the Lambo during lunch. Or they're going home to an empty life, an empty house, and an even emptier soul. Money can provide comfort, but it can't provide inner fulfillment.

I realized pretty early on that I didn't want that for my life. I'm not going to say it isn't nice to look out at Tampa from the 42nd floor of the Tampa Club with a glass of cabernet in your hand. It's just not *everything*.

Maybe it's because I grew up so poor that I never had that taste for luxury items. I'd much rather build a life that is financially comfortable so I can spend time with the people I love and take care of my family. That experience is more valuable to me than anything I could park in the garage.

But when Covid hit, I was suddenly the one who needed help instead of the one taking care of everybody else. I had to make a sudden U-turn, which could have been disastrous had I kept pretending everything was Armani-okay. Whether the help we need is physical, financial, or mental, it's okay to put up a hand and say, "I can't do this alone."

My mother struggled with her mental health. It took years to convince her to go to treatment. Once she did, her life was less stressful and she found more joy in each day. We all need some kind of help at some point in our lives, and it doesn't mean you are any less because you seek help. In fact, I think it means you are stronger than the person who keeps insisting everything is fine.

I couldn't do it by myself, and I'm glad I didn't have to. No one wants to get to the top of the ladder they worked so hard to climb and be there all alone. No one wants to reach their own personal Mt. Everest all by themselves. It's far more rewarding and fulfilling to look out at the world with someone you love by your side.

It's always better to be the crab at the top of the bucket than the one at the bottom, especially when the rest of the crabs lose their shit.

CHAPTER NINE
RICH DAD, POOR DAD, REBUILDING DAD

I lost my ass in 2020.

Not the one I sit on, but the one that pays the bills. My business took a huge nosedive when the Covid shutdowns started. It took three years to fix the damage the shutdown did to my bottom line and, if not for my husband, I would have lost my house. Yeah, it got that bad.

Not to mention, my mom was diagnosed with esophageal cancer in 2020, which only added to my stress and worry.

Up until then, my business had been very successful. When the pandemic hit, the world came to a stop. The international investments I had tanked. All of the work I had lined up ground to a complete halt and stayed that way for much, much longer than any of us expected.

My husband and I started cutting back; and when I say cutting back, I mean we trimmed away everything. Streaming services, subscriptions, ordering out—anything "extra" was gone. We got rid of our second car and dropped down to a one-car family, something I had never had to do before. We were struggling to get by on my husband's income alone, and that job got tougher and tougher every month.

In fact, more than once, I found myself in food distribution lines so I could bring home some free bread and milk to feed my son. I didn't want to be so prideful that I would turn my nose up at saving twenty bucks a week because every single dollar mattered.

I sank into a depression because I was just sitting at home for a year with nothing to do but watch everything I had worked so hard to build disappear. There were days I didn't want to get out of bed, but I did because I had to homeschool my son and help my mom. I realized later that a lot of that depression was actually grief. I was grieving the loss of a job and the loss of a company, although neither was entirely dead.

My world was essentially crumbling around me. The subcontractors I relied on took jobs elsewhere. I couldn't blame them as they had to feed their families, too. My partnership had dissolved, so it was just me and the company I had literally just started, TomCo Solutions. My name on the letterhead meant my name on the bottom line. I wasn't just starting at zero, I was starting at a negative number.

> **When you're starting over from a negative position, there's only one way to go—up.**

I began thinking maybe I should just get a nine-to-five. My husband said, "You haven't punched someone else's clock in so long, you'll be miserable doing it." He was right. I'd spent several years marching to the beat of my own drum and had no desire to get back on the rat race treadmill again.

Then there was the quarantine. I love my family dearly, but being stuck in a house with the same two people for months on end is not easy. I don't care how strong your relationship is, that kind of close quarters—with no break—is going to put a strain on your relationship.

As the months went by, people began to cautiously reinvest in building projects. By the end of 2020, work was starting to begin again for us and I began to feel some optimism.

Then in early 2021, I landed Zillow as a client. They had started Zillow Offers, a buy-and-flip operation. Someone who knew me recommended the company hire me to work on their flips. It was kind of eerie working for Zillow Offers because I never met a project manager. The Covid protocol was that the project manager came in prior to the start of a job and blue-taped or labeled whatever needed to be done. Then we would come in separately to avoid interactions. Because of Covid, we literally weren't allowed to be in the house at the same time.

For a while, it was just me and a handful of crew doing small jobs for Zillow Offers. I'd stock my car with the standard things I'd need from Home Depot and head out to Polk County to work on small projects. Subcontractors were hard to find at that time and more expensive (the old supply and demand rules). So, when I came in and changed out a smoke detector or hung a ceiling fan for a third of what they'd have to pay someone else (and faster than they could get someone else in to do the job), I looked like a hero—especially in rural areas where it was tougher to find help.

Even though things were going well with Zillow, I didn't want to put all of my eggs in one basket. I used my success with them to slowly build resources back up and take on other large clients as well. Things appeared to be back on track; I was still hurting but I could see the light at the end of the tunnel.

Then my mother got sicker. Some of the project managers were great to deal with, others not so much. One client had a PM that I will never forget. I talked to him on the phone and told him, "Hey, we're putting my mom in hospice today. I can't get back to you on that right now."

His response? "Here's the punch list of the items I need fixed. Take care of them."

No sympathy or empathy, no understanding; and for me, that was the beginning of the end for that. I have never been as disgusted with a human being as I was with that PM. It was the last job I took with that client.

Despite feeling a little relief that things were getting easier, I kept up with the financial reports on the news and began to see the writing on the wall for Zillow Offers. Interest rates were rising and housing sales were slowing. I think Zillow overpaid for a lot of their purchases to try to grab some of the market share. Combined with the costs for renovation skyrocketing because of supply issues, Zillow Offers was barely breaking even, or worse, losing money. It wasn't long before we all got an email saying they were shutting down that division.

Zillow Offers was my primary client at the time. Even though I expected it, the shutdown was pretty devastating. However, as the project managers I had worked for began to get jobs at other places, they'd recommend hiring me for a job and it didn't take long to get back to being busy. Many wonderful relationships with project managers at one company turned into many more wonderful relationships at multiple companies.

It was like going back to the beginning when I formed my first construction company. It was actually a nice way to grow my business because it made me feel like I was a brand-new entrepreneur all over again.

Then we had a problem of a different sort. Supply chain interruptions began to pile up, which had a big impact on my burgeoning business. I had a $30,000 job I couldn't close because of *one* shelf that wasn't available for months. Sometimes, we'd end up paying three or four times as much for materials than we had contracted because the shortages would drive up demand. Some clients worked with us on the extra costs; some didn't.

Throughout the pandemic shutdown, my mother underwent chemotherapy and she went into remission—for a while. My being unemployed was a blessing in disguise because it allowed me to be there with her when she needed help. Then, just as Zillow began shutting down, her cancer returned. Shortly after that, my mother died on August 22nd, 2022.

All over again, I sank into a depression. My mom was dead. My clients were going away. I was staring at another business precipice and felt like I was back at square one, or maybe even square negative one.

Then Hurricane Ian hit in the fall of 2022.

A few days after Hurricane Ian, I was set to host a charity pool party. A member of the group messaged me to say they needed to cancel their reservations for the event because a tree fell on their house. They sent me some pictures and all I wanted to do was help. "I'm a contractor," I said. "Do you want me to take a look and see what we can do?"

I have friends who work in insurance adjusting so I had mentors to help me understand the billing process for storm damage. That allowed me to help them get their paperwork squared away so they could deal with the tree in the middle of their house. Right after that job, I picked up another lead on a hurricane-damaged house and suddenly had $500,000 worth of work.

That job led to another, then another. Before the hurricane, I was doing twenty jobs a month but all of them at low profit margins. I was working, which was great, but I was exhausted and knew something was going to have to change because I was beginning to feel more like a dog chasing his own tail than a successful company owner.

The opportunity to help homeowners devastated by Hurricane Ian changed the course of my business. I was now able to focus on fewer, higher-margin jobs. This made a massive difference in my business.

> Remember what I said about doing the math? It's like a giant barometer for where your business stands.

And whoop-whoop, no need to go back into the regular workforce. Probably a very good thing for me because I'd much rather watch that than live it. My favorite ride at Disney is the Carousel of Progress at Magic Kingdom, which is an antiquated, George Jetson-type version of how our world has changed. In one part of the ride, you see all the people driving to and from work. The announcer calls them rats in the rat race. That was how those twenty jobs a month felt, and I knew that wasn't what I wanted. That meant another shift in my business, but I had just weathered a pretty massive one so I knew I would be okay.

What really got me through Covid, though, was the support of the people around me. My husband was amazing. He supported us, he was patient and understanding, and he provided the safety net I needed in order to go back into business for myself. Then I have friends like Gary, who is a high school teacher who always says, "You can do it, you're going to be big, I just know it." (Hey Gary, now you can tell your students that Mr. Carlson has been mentioned in a book!)

Not everyone is like that, and I understand because we're all conditioned from birth to get a reliable job with an insurance plan and a 401k. My grandmother is one of those people who believes the safest thing to do with your money is put it in the bank.

She's the one who always says, "Be careful, Tommy, don't get hurt." I get that she wants to protect me from the inevitable storms and turbulence of life. But if I'd never taken a risk, never had a loss, and—most of all—never failed, I wouldn't be where I am today.

When Grandma says that, I give her a hug, assure her it will all be fine, and then take the leap anyway. Because you can't get where you want to go by sitting on your ass.

Surviving 2020 was harder than assembling IKEA furniture without instructions or tools.

CHAPTER TEN
THE REAL PROBLEMS ARE UNDER THE DRYWALL

There's one thing I learned pretty damned fast in the construction world: You never know what you're going to find behind the drywall, and I mean that in every possible way. We've dealt with illegal wiring that wasn't connected to any kind of electrical panel, plumbing that has been leaking for years, termite damage that left the wall a shell of itself, and secret rooms built before the Depression.

I wish there was an MRI for houses so we could see everything behind the walls before we give a client an estimate on time and materials. While I try to figure in costs for the most common problems we deal with, no one expects to tear down a wall and find…

A moonshine-making operation.

Seriously. That's exactly what we found. We were working on a house in New Port Richey and, as we looked at the measurements we took of the outside of the house and the ones we took of the interior rooms, the math didn't quite add up. There was an extra, unaccounted-for space. When we tore down one of the walls, we found an entire still operation that had been boarded up. I'd love to know the story behind the still, but sadly, this was a foreclosure that came to us with no history from the previous owners.

And, no free moonshine. I know, bummer on all counts.

Another time, we were opening the walls of an apartment that had a super high moisture content. While we expected to find mold and wood rot, we did *not* expect to see live snakes and frogs. There they were, right behind the drywall, slithering and jumping the second we opened up the wall. That was a day my guys won't soon forget.

There are cool things we've found, too, things that are almost like a time capsule to a bygone era, like turn-of-the-century horseshoes or old newspapers. There are also not-cool things, like a string dangling under a sink that turned out to be a giant rat.

I can't bid on what I can't see, but I can make reasonable estimations based on the age and condition of the house. Some people call me pessimistic when I note probable water damage, electrical work, or plumbing replacements, but I prefer to consider it being pragmatic. It's far better to anticipate these problems than suddenly spring them on the client. The more you know ahead of time, the more heartache you save yourself—in business and in life.

People, I've found, are a lot like drywall. They can be perfect on the outside—a nice satin finish, no blemishes—but beneath that shiny exterior can be a person you didn't expect. I like to figure out what kind of person you are pretty early on in the process and I have a (sort of) foolproof method of weeding out the people I don't want to be friends with:

I tell a slightly off-color joke and see how they respond.

I'm not talking late-night HBO kind of jokes, but something just a little on the inappropriate side. Some people are cool and laugh. Others get indignant. And a few expose their own inner hatred, racism, and judgment.

> Those people are not my people.

I'll also get a little personal because I've found that being a little vulnerable (or a lot, considering everything I've divulged in this book) helps other people open up, too. They begin to feel a connection, and from that connection comes trust. When people trust you, they want to get to know you better, do more business with you, and send more business your way.

It's a quid-pro-quo world, though, and when I get to know and like someone, I do what I can to help them out, whether that's writing a referral letter or giving them business advice.

I don't do that because I must—I do it because I know, like, and trust these people and I want to see them succeed. On top of that, I respect their ability to ask for help or admit they're struggling, and that makes me want to help even more. It's incredibly brave to open up and show your inner self to someone else. No one should ever take advantage of that kind of vulnerability.

Which also means sometimes keeping your mouth shut. If you tell me a secret or something about yourself that you don't share with many people, I'll never repeat it. I'm not opening up your personal drywall for you—that's your decision.

Covid exposed vulnerabilities in so many of us. I know lots of people who lost their shirts in 2020, myself included. There are so many who are still trying to climb out of the hole Covid threw them into. When I see someone struggling, I want to be first in line to give them a helping hand. I'm not so proud that I won't admit I went to a food bank during Covid (just re-read Chapter 9 to see why), and you shouldn't be either. It's only in these kinds of commonalities that we build bridges with each other.

Listen, I know poverty. I know struggle. My first suit came from Goodwill, for Pete's sake. It was a decent suit, blue with gold buttons, and it did the job. I've worked my butt off to get to the point where I can afford to have a custom suit made. I tell you this, not because I want to gloat about my ability to afford a tailor, but to say to all those kids living in a trailer on a glorified piece of dirt: *I made it, and you can too.*

> Watch out for the leeches and vampires who want to use your optimism and trust for their own gain. Those kinds of people take and take, and never put anything back in the universe. They're drainers, not givers.

How do you know who to trust and who to back away from? Try the Galvanic Skin Response.[1] If you've never heard of this, it's basically some pretty cool science that talks about the "tells" we all have that give another person a hint as to what kind of person we are. Your body gives off a billion details without you even knowing. From a sweaty handshake to an avoidant gaze, learning to read these clues in other people can save you a lot of wasted time.

Maybe it comes from the trauma in my childhood, which kept me on guard and always ready to respond to a crisis, but I can immediately tell if someone is the type of person I want to work with based on the pitch of their voice or their stance. Closed-off people make me uncomfortable, because I'm always leery there's some personality snake just waiting in the bush to strike.

If I see a red flag, or heck, a hint of a yellow flag, I walk away. Sadly, people aren't as easily repaired as a plumbing issue

---

1 https://www.sciencedirect.com/topics/computer-science/galvanic-skin-response

behind the drywall. Science has come a long way, but they haven't yet managed to create an MRI that can show you what's behind the walls of houses—or people.

Success is in your mind, not your bank account.

CHAPTER ELEVEN
STUDY THE HAMBURGERS ON YOUR SPREADSHEET

In case it isn't obvious by now, I love me a spreadsheet, with all its data points and analysis opportunities. You would think that someone like me, a closet accountant, would think the numbers are always right.

They aren't.

Sometimes the numbers don't paint the true picture. You might think what you're seeing is good news, but if you dig a little deeper, you'll realize that's not the case. When I started up again after Covid, I was flooded with job contracts for $50,000, $60,000, even $70,000. That year, my company grossed over a million dollars.

I should have been ecstatic. A million dollars? That's *fantastic* for a new company. Yet, as I looked around, I didn't see the profits I thought I'd have from a million dollars. I didn't feel as financially secure as I thought I would with seven figures on the general ledger.

That's because the numbers, on the outside, were lying to me.

When I dove deep into the numbers, I realized the margins on those jobs, which had seemed lucrative when we were hustling to get them done, weren't good. In fact, my margins were astronomically low. So, while we were booking jobs and busier than ever, we were almost losing money because I was killing myself to bring in those dollars.

At the time, it was just me and a few subcontractors. I didn't have an assistant or any kind of staff yet to help lighten the load. Even if I had, I couldn't have afforded them with margins like that. Conventional wisdom says that I should have had at least $100,000 profit leftover from that million dollars. I definitely did not make that much of a profit.

So, what went wrong?

I had the quantity of numbers, but I didn't have the *quality* of numbers. There's a big difference between the two. Jobs that have quality numbers are ones where I'm making a profit that sustains the business and helps it grow. As much as I'd love to help every person that comes to me with a job, the reality is not every job is the right one for me.

Some of those bad numbers came from the rollercoaster of construction costs that happened after Covid. One job that was waiting on a bunch of wire shelves—small pieces that normally cost less than twenty bucks—was held up for months. The shelves were not only backordered, but the price had gone up to almost *two hundred dollars*. Each. For. A. Shelf.

That kind of insanity is going to eat into your profits pretty fast.

It was tempting, especially in those early days, to hear a client say, "I can bring you hundreds of these types of jobs" and see that as a path to dependable income. I had to have the courage to step back, run the numbers, and realize that the high quantity jobs were only going to put me further and further behind profit-wise.

> **I need to make money on every single job, not just some of them.**

And I started turning them down. I'm not going to lie, that was pretty terrifying the first few times. Often, I'll explain to the person that the margins simply aren't good enough for me. If I can't make enough to keep the lights on at TomCo, it doesn't make sense to do that work.

I've had investors come to me and say, "I can't believe it's going to cost that much to do this job. That's above my budget. I paid two hundred thousand for this house and need to make fifty thousand on the sale."

My answer to that is some variation of: "I understand, but I am a contractor, not a real estate investor. That's the risk you take when you flip property. Not every deal is going to be profitable." The one constant in real estate investing is that some projects are going to lose money. The market is constantly fluctuating and it's easy to overpay for a house at the height of the market, then lose money selling it later. Hence, why I am not in the real estate business.

Once I realized my million dollars wasn't as great a thing as I'd thought, I went back to my old friend, Excel. There was no way I was going to lose another two hundred dollars to a wire shelf.

I broke down every single step of every single job and costed it all out, just as I had costed out hamburgers at the resort. I created a matrix that helped me see at a glance what a job would cost me in labor, supplies, payroll, the inevitable holdups, etc. The margins were there in black and white, so it was an easy decision to raise prices when needed or turn down jobs that didn't work out on the spreadsheet.

When a client balked, I had the evidence to show why the job would cost that much. The clients didn't always like the price increases, but they understood them and realized I was just trying to make money, like they were. What's more, because I essentially opened the numbers to them, they trusted me and knew I wasn't going to overcharge them.

I was also clearly running my business in a way that meant I was in it for the long haul. There are dozens of fly-by-night contractors in this area and, from the day I started, that fact has meant working a little bit harder to earn a client's trust and long-term business. I'm honest and upfront with them, and that goes a long way in a business relationship. By being able to show them, "Hey, doing the job at this price is not sustainable and, if I'm losing money, I'll be out of business and not here to do the job," I can justify what I have to charge to do the work.

Yes, there were the few who whispered, "Why not use unlicensed labor and save a few bucks?" That was never even a consideration for me. If I use unlicensed labor and something goes wrong, I'm the one who loses my contractor's license—and my business. Why would I put my entire livelihood at risk for such low margins?

Around the same time I was doing all those calculations, Florida was hit by Hurricane Ian and that dropped some insurance restoration projects in my lap. When I looked at my trusty spreadsheet, I realized I was making more on those two projects than I had on twenty projects the year before. Yes, it took longer to complete those projects, but the margins were better and that meant long-term sustainability for my company.

When you analyze the hamburgers on your spreadsheets, you stop chasing the little stuff to pay the bills. The more I did that, the more I could see the path toward the projects I actually wanted to work on, which has brought me to a whole different category of clients.

> **Not chasing after dozens of jobs gives you room to breathe. To think. To plan your next step.**

Don't take a job just because you need money in the bank account. Doing that will keep you too busy to go after the jobs you really want, the ones that will take your business to the next level. I get it, a lot of us have to do the 60-80-100-hour weeks in the beginning just to keep the lights on. But at a certain point, it's worth it to step back and say...

Is that hamburger really worth the cost?

Keeping your head in the sand is a risky business strategy—the ostrich may avoid eye contact at the risk of suffocation!

CHAPTER TWELVE
THERE IS POWER IN YOUR NETWORK

It was time to do something different.

Those who know me would say I've always done things differently (ha ha), but business-wise, I needed to get out of my rut and *get out of the house*. I love my family, I truly do, but Covid and all its quarantine closeness really, really tested those bonds.

My mother's passing left me feeling a little adrift, too. And I think that, coupled with emerging from quarantine and restarting my business, made me crave building more professional connections. Someone suggested I try networking. Really? A contractor at a networking meeting? Wasn't that kind of thing just for lawyers and financial advisors?

"Come to a BNI meeting," someone said. "You'll love it."

BNI, also known as Business Network International, seemed (from the outside) like one of those stuffy, conservative groups. It's been around since the mid 80s and has chapters in more than seventy countries; so clearly, it works. Still, I resisted for a long time because I thought going to one of these meetings would mean going back in the closet. Then I saw a posting in a gay professionals group on Facebook for a local BNI meeting and thought, *Hmm, maybe this group isn't as stuffy as I thought.*

I'd been marketing to individuals at events and on LinkedIn for a long time, and while that was definitely leading to work, I realized I also needed help growing my business and making connections with people who "got" me and the challenges I faced as an entrepreneur.

I went to that first meeting on a Tuesday morning and immediately realized this was the place for me. I was right, there were a lot of lawyers and financial advisors in the group and not a lot of trades people, but the approach that BNI took—concentrating on business growth, not just referrals—was unique and something I needed at the time.

Every Tuesday morning when I sit down at my local BNI meeting, I devote that time to giving my business serious thought. The advice, conversations, and connections I've made there have helped me level up a little more every time.

I'm surprised I don't see more people in the construction industry participating in networking. Where else can you go in a major city like Tampa to make connections with the type of people who are likely to work with you or buy services from you? What's more, there are dozens of professionals in every meeting that have become more than just referral partners—they're friends.

I get that construction is a feast or famine industry. Contractors will always take time to put out fires because those equal a paycheck. They'll go through periods where they're slammed and times when they haven't worked in almost a month.

Here's the thing about networking: It's not about hunting for the next client. It's about farming the soil and planting those seeds of connection that will eventually blossom into steady work.

> If you don't take time to plant the seeds by networking, your business won't reap a bountiful harvest.

When you go to a meeting, you should look like you belong there. No paint-stained shorts and flip-flops. I'm not saying you have to put on that too-small suit from your wedding. A nice polo shirt and some khakis works just fine. I have some company-branded ones that I wear to events and networking meetings. It's an easy way for people to recognize who I am and what I do without having to hand out a business card every five seconds. When I want to get fancy, I opt for the company-branded white long-sleeved dress shirt and a blueprint-patterned tie that has tools on it. For *really* fancy events, I have a light-up bow tie that I can color coordinate with my suit. With that kind of game, I'm surprised Christian Dior isn't asking me for fashion advice.

That's about as fancy as I get for the Tampa Club, too. I joined the club early in 2023 and was impressed with the environment. It's a city club filled with professionals, not a pretentious leather-lined drawing room full of people playing pinochle. I could just as easily go to Starbucks to have breakfast, but it's far more productive for me to eat breakfast on the 42nd floor and connect with people who are in my customer demographic.

The heart of networking is in the connection. Done right, it can transform your business. My best networking tips are easy but also effective:

- Be friendly to everyone. You don't have to be Norm in *Cheers,* but you should show a genuine interest in everyone you meet.
- Ask the easy questions. Break the ice with a simple, "What do you do?" and let other people talk about themselves instead of leaping in to talk about

you. "Me, me, me" doesn't work any better at a networking event than it does in regular interactions.

- Be a nerd. Ask questions about other industries, get interested in how they work. My interest in aquariums brought me to the Florida Aquarium and an introduction to its Director of Philanthropy. It goes back to the farming analogy—never stop meeting people because you never know when that will pan out. I have not only made a new friend, but I now partner with a wonderful organization that I first visited as a child.
- Don't sell all the damned time. Nobody likes that. Period.
- Support good causes and good people. *Just because.* When I saw a news report about how the beads from Gasparilla parades damage the Tampa waterways, I made a quick video reminding people not to throw them in the bay. I didn't get anything from that. I wasn't trying to schmooze anyone. I just did it because it's the right thing to do.
- Host events and people will come to you. Plus, you get to control the microphone, which is always fun. I hosted a behind-the-scenes event at the Florida Aquarium that had nothing to do with sales. It was all about bonding between the select group of people I invited, all while helping an amazing cause.
- Be grateful for every referral. I get some (a lot) of referrals that don't work out for one reason or

another. Nonetheless, I always thank the person who referred me because they went out of their way to think of me and create a connection.
- Go into every meeting with a focus on giving to others, not getting for yourself. Whether it's a referral, advice, or simply a supportive shoulder, starting with giving is always a good thing. I've solved problems in my company by helping someone else solve theirs. Taking the focus off what I had going on allowed me to see my own issues in a different way.

One more thing: You literally never know who you're going to meet or when you're going to meet them, so always show up as your best self. The first time I met Yasmine Gardiner was at a Tampa Club networking event. She told me she was a data scientist (that was awesome, because, as a fellow nerd, I love nerds!) and she had on a blouse that showed off her full-sleeve tattoos. I remember thinking, *Wow, she is a badass nerd!*

Then my husband and I ran into her again at a cooking class. Because neither of us was pressing for a sale, we ended up having great conversations and becoming great friends. Now I know, like, and trust her, so I was delighted when she asked me to partner with her on an exciting new venture in AI. That connection fed into my goal of being a disruptor in the construction industry (you'll have to keep reading to see how and why) and of connecting with a whole lot more people that love data almost as much as I do.

Start with the host, not the hors d'oeuvres, at a networking event because the host knows everyone can create those warm introductions.

CHAPTER THIRTEEN
JUST BECAUSE YOU'RE FORTY DOESN'T MEAN YOU KNOW WHAT YOU'RE DOING

I timed this book to be released around my 40th birthday for a few reasons: I like an excuse to throw a kickass party; I wanted to check off another bucket list item before this milestone birthday; and it's a creative way to make watching The Rocky Horror Picture Show into a tax deduction. Yes, you can hire me for business consulting advice if you are thinking of hosting a Dune launch party. Just kidding. Sort of.

Back to the birthday. Forty. Even when I say that word out loud, I'm thinking, *Wow. Forty? Really? Me? Already?*

When I was a kid, I thought forty was *old*. My mom was so young when she had me that my grandmother was only thirty-seven when I was born. She wasn't even fifty by the time I was a teenager, but she was a granny. In my eyes, that was one step away from being the Crypt Keeper.

Then I got through my thirties and realized forty-year-olds are not that much more equipped for life than I was at eighteen. Racking up a pile of birthdays doesn't instantly give you answer-knowing superpowers. A lot of us are still fumbling around, doing the best we can. We're just wearing a nice suit and pretending we're not lost.

I'm right on the edge of being a millennial. I grew up with encyclopedias, not iPads; and I used an atlas to get around because GPS didn't exist. Remember those TripTik Planners from AAA? I do! They were the MapQuest of my generation. I'm probably dating myself by even using the word MapQuest. TripTik Planners were basically step by step directions printed on a handheld paper map that could be flipped like a small spiral notebook; which, to those of us still hauling out a road atlas to get to Orlando, was pretty darned cool.

The world has changed a bit since TripTiks. Gen Z is used to having everything they need at their fingertips. Instant information, instant food delivery, instant directions. They are less patient (although that could just be the grumpy old man in me saying that. And yes, sometimes I have the urge to yell at people to get off my lawn).

The cool thing about being not-quite-forty, though, is that you're still young enough for younger people to see you as someone who is kinda cool and has some knowledge, while older people respect you because you've paid your dues. Most of the time.

There's an episode of *The Simpsons*, the source of all knowledge (only sort of kidding) where Lisa says, "It's awful being a kid. No one listens to ya."

"It's rotten being old," Grandpa Simpson replies. "No one listens to ya."

Homer walks in on the conversation and says, "I'm a white male, aged eighteen to forty-nine. Everyone listens to me, no matter how dumb my suggestions are."

File that under things that are sad but true.

But, if you have the experience and wisdom to back up your words, that makes a difference. Recently, I had a conversation with a young business person. He was in his mid-twenties. As I gave him advice, I could see that he was listening hard to every single word that came out of my mouth, as if I was giving him the best business advice of his life. I was thinking, *Wow, maybe I do know a thing or two.*

I have people who work for me who are almost a full generation older than I am. They have experience I don't yet have and, even though they work for me, I'll listen when they come up with a solution because I know they have years of doing that thing behind their ideas. There are others who are all bluster and no game, but if you pay attention, you can pick them out pretty quickly.

Covid, as devastating as it was for most businesses, had one good side effect—it encouraged us to be more vulnerable with each other. Almost *everyone* was hurt in some way by the pandemic, and almost every business saw an impact on their bottom line.

> Nowadays, admitting that you had a massive setback during 2020 is okay no matter how old, experienced, or savvy you are.

We all get it because we all went through the same exact thing. All that wisdom and experience couldn't prepare any of us for what happened that year. Heck, I don't think a single person in the world was truly prepared for 2020.

The lesson in that? People can be smart and get hit with bad circumstances. They can be successful and still experience massive failure. Turning forty—or fifty, or any other age—doesn't come with a no-mistakes guarantee.

Good to know, right? Takes a lot of the pressure off. When I screw up, I'll just say, "I'm forty. It happens."

That's essentially what Cord Christensen, the founder and CEO of PetIQ, said at a conference I recently attended. Christensen began his company in 2009 after receiving a high vet bill that made him wonder if there was a way to sell pet medications for less money. He started PetIQ, then began manufacturing generic versions of popular medications and selling them in major retailers. He was only in his thirties when he started the company. He's now in his early fifties and the company is valued at a billion dollars.

Before there was a PetIQ, though, Christensen had worked for and partnered with a guy named Tom Petters, at Petters Co. Inc. Petters ran a brokerage firm that was going gangbusters, offering steady returns of 15-20%.

Anyone familiar with Bernie Madoff knows where this is going.

Petters was fudging the numbers and spending the money from investors as fast as it came in, playing a very good financial shell game. Christensen had no idea. He invested $2 million of his own money and convinced others to invest another $2 million in Petters' company shortly before he left to start PetIQ.

The FBI got wind of what was going on, and they raided Petters' room at the Bellagio and his corporate offices near the end of 2008. Petters was convicted, went to jail, and never repaid the money.

Christensen told this story, admitting that his business partner had played him for a fool and stolen half of what he had to his name at the time. *Half.* Lawyers told Christensen that little, if any, of the money would ever be recovered. So Christensen let it go, moved on, and started his own company.

> If you haven't quite made it yet, no matter what age you are, that's okay. There are no rules that say you have to hit this level by a certain age. Here's the truth "old" people don't tell you—we're all still trying to figure it out.

After he told this story, I stood up to ask a question. "You're the only CEO here that has talked about failure. What made you go on and start your own company instead of just going to work for someone else?"

Christensen looked at me with all seriousness in his face. "I couldn't get a job, so I had no choice but to succeed on my own." He'd been in his thirties and starting from nothing after being burned, learning a powerful lesson about failure and trust. I admired his raw honesty because it lets the rest of us know we don't have to get it right on the first try (just like I didn't).

There are dozens of people who didn't start hitting their strides until their forties, like Oprah, Stan Lee, and Sam

Walton. That tells me there are great things on the horizon after my birthday.

Well, after I recover from my birthday party, that is.

There is no magic age for having all your shit together.

CHAPTER FOURTEEN
THAT RANDOM TRIVIA IS GOOD FOR MORE THAN JEOPARDY

My head is filled with useless trivia. I can tell you the tip of a shoe lace is called an aglet and a group of Flamingos is called a flamboyance, neither of which is actually useful information.

Until you're on a job site and you're trying to figure out how to waterproof a garage without tearing it down.

I've had a variety of jobs in finance, accounting, hospitality, and retail. I've worked in pretty much every major facet of Corporate America. You wouldn't think that information would come in handy in a trade industry but it does, more often than you'd believe.

That's probably why I run my business a lot differently than other contractors. Calming down a resort guest whose reservation had been double-booked requires a lot of the same skills as calming down a homeowner whose garage is filling with water. You want people to know that you hear them, that you understand why they are upset, and that they are reacting to having some portion of their life upended. That allows you to create a bond with the customer, making them more receptive to the solution…which may not be perfect.

You don't have to become best friends and tell ghost stories around a campfire, but you do have to build empathy. Shrugging someone off when they are genuinely upset is disrespectful and will eventually cost you your clientele.

If you think about it, hospitality is the perfect industry to develop the soft skills every business owner needs. Someone who is staying at a hotel or resort is looking for a respite from the problems of their life. When things go wrong, they lose that sense of relaxation. All of a sudden, they're smack-dab in the middle of a pile of problems again.

When we renovate a home, we are invading and tearing apart someone's personal space. We are taking away their safe space and promising them that we'll put it back better than it was before. I tell every one of my clients, "You might like me now, but there is going to come a point where you hate me."

"Never," they reply. That's because they're still in the dating phase of a home renovation.

After the first few weeks, when the honeymoon wears off and their house is a dusty, gaping wreck, the clients inevitably get frustrated, then scared that their home will never look beautiful again. "It's all going to work out," I reassure them. "We'll get through this together."

By taking the time to listen to their concerns, address them, and maybe go the extra mile, I'm doing the same thing as when I'd bring a disgruntled guest a free margarita or ask housekeeping to fold the towels into elephant shapes because the guest's kids love elephants.

> Those two things—listening and paying attention to the small details—will do more to build strong customer relationships than anything else you do.

Sometimes, you need more than a margarita or a towel. You need a creative answer to solve a problem. Like a subterranean garage filling with ground water. It had been built directly under the main house, which meant we'd have to tear it all down to fix this problem. Obviously, the clients didn't want to spend hundreds of thousands of dollars to fix the garage.

I thought about the resort and repairs we had to make to the pool one time. The contractor had brought in marcite and used it to patch the leaks in the pool. Marcite, a blend of cement and marble dust, is durable, waterproof, and paintable.

I called a pool vendor and asked him to shoot marcite on the walls of the garage. Astounded, he blurted, "You want me to do what?!"

My team put drains into the floor of the garage, the pool guy covered the walls with marcite, and we painted them to match the garage. And it worked. That off-label use of a pool product blocked the water intrusion in the garage.

Random trivia for the win!

The first people to embrace out-of-the-box thinking were mimes. If it can work for people just pretending to be stuck, imagine what it could do for your business.

CHAPTER FIFTEEN
WELP, THAT SHIT'S GONNA FAIL

Around the same time as Zillow Offers closed their doors and I was scrambling to find business, I read 10x is Easier than 2x by Benjamin Hardy and Dan Sullivan. The 10x book made me think long and hard about where I put my energy and how that affected my success. The basic premise of Hardy and Sullivan's book is: Get rid of the 80% of your day that wears you down, makes you miserable, and has a low return on investment, so you can concentrate on the 20% you love and that has exponential profit potential.

Cutting out any part of your business when you are an entrepreneur who's counting every penny is terrifying. Plus, when you're the head honcho, it's really, really easy to get swept up into the minutiae of your company. There's a lot of things coming across your desk and the boss in you thinks you need to know what all those papers say, but here's the truth:

> You don't need to be weighed down by the little shit.

I'm sure you didn't go into business to deal with all the little crap. Most people don't. In the beginning, when your business is still getting off the ground, you do have to do everything because you don't have the income to justify hiring help. But once your company begins to grow, it's time to make a choice:

Are you going to hire people to handle the little shit or are you still going to keep trying to do it all?

The 10x book talks about doing the things that you love, that you excel at doing, and that you see as your best path to mega-success. By concentrating on that 20% and letting the other 80% go, you are using every minute more efficiently, thus growing your business faster.

It seems counterintuitive, right? Let go of 80% of what is bringing in money for your business just to hold tighter to the 20%?

It was a tough lesson for me to learn, especially when it came to all those spreadsheets I love so much. I am happy as a clam digging into data all day, but that is not where my passions lie. It's not what I've dreamed of doing or the vision I've had from the day I opened TomCo Solutions. So as much as it pained me, I had to let go of the spreadsheets and *gasp*! hire a fractional CFO to come in and do that data scrubbing for me.

I know. I needed a hug that day.

I could see, though, that my own pride and human fallacies were holding me and my business back from growing the way it should. I also took some time to really nail down the 20% that drove me to get out of bed every day.

> **Sometimes you gotta let go to get ahead.**

Besides running TomCo Solutions, I love nonprofit work. I love connecting people. I love speaking and communicating my message. None of those other things were contracting work, but they were things that I was passionate about.

In order to have time to do it all, I also had to hire a Director of Construction Operations so I wasn't spending every hour of my day going from site to site, making sure the punch list got checked off. When I took away doing the drywall orders and scheduling the plumbers, it gave me more time for business development. I had the hours (and sometimes weeks) to build relationships that net multi-million-dollar projects rather than spending the whole day chasing a bunch of small ones.

Because I had more time for business development, I had more time to think, plan, and listen to other people. I could step back and have that eagle's view of my business. Entrepreneurs tend to be people who like to think and dream big. You can't do that if you're busy juggling ten thousand balls at once.

My Director of Construction loves what he does. In fact, he's probably better at it than I am. He does not love doing what I do—networking, speaking, etc. When we each stay in the lanes we love, we are more productive and much, much happier. I wake up every morning excited to get to work and see what the day has in store for me. What connections I can make. What businesses I can help. And how I can tackle bigger and bigger goals, like growing my private equity firm and building affordable housing for underserved communities.

When I decided to take the 10x approach and began telling people about it, I could see the doubt in their eyes. The "Well, that shit's gonna fail" look they gave me, and sometimes said aloud. If the people around you are sowing seeds of doubt in your ear—

Find new people.

I'm serious. Being an entrepreneur is hard enough. There are a ton of responsibilities, worries, and expectations on your shoulders. The last thing you need is someone telling you that you're gonna fall flat on your face.

I get it; they're just trying to save you some heartache or give you a preview of the future. I remember my mom telling me, "One of these days, you're going to have a son and you'll see how hard it is to be a parent." She was right; there are certain experiences you can only learn from by going through it yourself.

But that doesn't mean you need to fail or that you are destined to fail. Failure starts in your head. So, if you start thinking that way, it will inevitably happen. There's a pie out there, but it doesn't have a finite number of pieces. We can all have a piece; we just have to believe that the piece exists.

It's a sad day when you realize your mom was right. But it's an even sadder day when she's not here for you to tell her that.

CHAPTER SIXTEEN
THERE'S MORE TO BUSINESS THAN MONEY

Some days, running your own business feels a lot like trying to plug twenty holes in the Hoover Dam, all at the same time, and with just a single package of chewing gum. When you're an entrepreneur, and people (like your family) are depending on you to make a go of the business and keep a roof over their heads, it's tough to focus on anything other than the money coming in and the money going out.

When things got rough, I could have curled up into a ball and spent my days watching *Schitt's Creek* reruns and eating Funyuns. That sounded like a pretty good idea when my business came to a screeching halt and our income dropped by 80% while the world was running out of Clorox wipes.

I'm not going to say I never had a Funyuns day, but I didn't spend a lot of time wallowing or bemoaning the situation. All that would do was make things worse. And make my family very upset. All around me, I saw people who had it worse than we did. People who had no one to help them. People in dire financial straits. People who were stranded and scared.

To take my mind off myself, I decided to delve into nonprofit work. I joined a social group of people who felt the same and who had a similar need to make an impact for the people around us. They wanted to increase the number of charitable actions that they did each year but needed help with their board. I joined the board and helped facilitate their fundraising efforts (if there's one thing I love, it's planning a party!).

We raised tens of thousands of dollars in the aftermath of the shutdown, simply by hosting fun events for people. All these charities that had lost donations because of the pandemic were able to recoup some of those losses because of this group's support.

I stayed on the board for two years; and when I finally stepped down, I realized I had used all that nonprofit work as a way to distract myself from my mom's cancer and eventual death, and the impact of 2020 on my business. It allowed me to focus on things outside my own heartbreak, which was both good and bad because it delayed the inevitable emotional wall I hit.

That didn't mean that I wanted to stop volunteering, though. I think that *everyone* should find time to volunteer with something that impacts the community. I don't care how busy you are, you have to do something that gives back because it's the right thing to do. It also sends a strong message when a busy professional makes a nonprofit a priority.

If you aren't that selfless (and heck, most of us aren't), then do it because charity work gives back to you as well. It can raise your profile in the community, yes, but leaves you with a significant level of gratitude and satisfaction that is almost impossible to find anywhere else.

I do much more nonprofit work than most people even realize because I rarely post about it on social media. I'm not there to grab a quick selfie to prove I'm a do-gooder. I'm there because my heart wants me to be.

When I do post on social media, it's to give wider exposure to a small charity that might not have the opportunity (or marketing budget) to reach many people. For instance, I made a post about an auction I attended at a local animal sanctuary. I wasn't showing off the cool retro cat shirt I bought (it was very cool though); I was highlighting the awesome work a local charity was doing. Maybe the post got them one more follower, one more donor, or one more adopter of a pet needing a forever home. It cost me nothing to make that post.

You can donate your expertise if you don't have a lot of time. If you are a whiz at financials or a turnaround specialist, you can use those skills with a nonprofit. Chances are good the nonprofit would never be able to afford to hire someone with your level of experience or expertise, so volunteering to sit on the board or just consulting with them can make a huge difference.

There have been multiple organizations that I've served as the bookkeeper or treasurer to help when they're overwhelmed with their financials. I go in there and help them get everything set up and automated, do the tedious work of allocating expenses in their books, help them create a budget, and do predictive modeling for the future. It's a few hours of work for me, but it can save the nonprofit dozens of hours.

Also think about cross-connecting the communities you serve. We're all there for the same purpose—to give back and help others—so why not multiply your efforts together? For example, I was part of a charity that had a religious component. They were doing a shoe drive for foster children and refugees. I went to the LGBTQ+ charity I was involved with and said, "Hey, this is a good cause. Why don't we try to raise money and shoes for this group?"

We held an event and asked everybody who came to either bring a pair of shoes to give away or donate $20. We brought in dozens of pairs of shoes—and raised $2000. Two thousand dollars buys a lot of shoes! I went into a value retail store and told the manager what we were doing. The manager had five associates help me find the best shoes for the money we had. We bought all the clearance shoes in the store, and then made sure we bought plenty of shoes for boys and girls of all ages. In addition to that, the manager gave us a 10% discount on the purchase, which made our money stretch even further.

I ended up buying *two hundred* pairs of shoes. The charity was shocked and grateful when I walked in with all those boxes!

Word got out about what we were doing, and I was contacted by someone who had things to donate. Turns out it was shoes and women's undergarments that were meant to be sold to the state prison system, but the prisons had changed their guidelines so these items no longer worked. The company wanted to get them out of their warehouse and offered to donate all of them to us.

We received $30,000 worth of undergarments and shoes. The donation was so big (more than 2000 pairs of shoes!), we had to rent a U-Haul to get it over to the nonprofit's office.

All this came just from connecting some dots between people in the community, for no reason other than to help. The largest takeaway is that it didn't cost me anything to do this. I just made some social media posts about the donation drive and boom, a life-changing donation was made to hundreds of families. It was just a handful of us who banded together and provided this amazing gift for others.

> A small group of people can make a massive difference.

After that, people who remembered me from the group would refer me to anyone looking for a contractor. Literally, they introduced me to people left and right. I didn't do it for the introductions. I did it to help these kids and refugees who needed our support.

When I talk to another entrepreneur or a budding business person, I ask them where they are volunteering. A lot of them say they are too busy. My answer is, "What are you passionate about? Because when you get involved with something that you are passionate about, it's easy to find the time." If those interests align with a group I know, I'll make the introduction for them.

Nonprofit work also creates this kind of permanent network of amazing people. Your next employer could be at a nonprofit event right now. Your next girlfriend, boyfriend, fiancé, husband, wife, or business partner is probably at a nonprofit event right now. When you go and volunteer, put in your time, genuinely get to know other people who care about the same causes as you do, you'll find that you are dealing with a better caliber of person who shares the same values.

For me, the thing I am most passionate about is building affordable housing for underserved communities. The passion for that kind of charity work goes right back to my childhood. My husband also grew up poor. Years ago, we started volunteering with Toys for Tots, but it wasn't enough. I wanted to make a bigger difference.

Anyone who has looked at real estate in Florida knows that "affordable" and "housing" are two words that don't go together. Prices are skyrocketing and the cost is getting out of control for so many people.

> When a kid falls asleep in school, it's often because they didn't get a good night's sleep at home the night before. School is a safe place for them to sleep. All kids deserve to have a home where they feel safe enough, warm enough, and secure enough to get a good night's sleep.

So many children are struggling in school and in life because they do not have a reliable home situation. Maybe there's lead paint on the walls, or rodents everywhere, or gunshots going off in the street. Those kids did nothing to deserve that kind of life. They deserve a good night's sleep. They deserve to feel safe within the walls around them.

You never know if that kid will be the next one to cure cancer or become president or find a way to world peace. Because of that, I don't want to just help fifty families or a hundred families, I want to help thousands of families.

Yes, that's an ambitious goal. And very likely not one that will make me a billionaire, but if we don't give back to the world around us, what are we doing here?

For now, I'm concentrating on affordable housing for particular subset groups like homeless people, veterans, and LGBTQ+. Up until just a few years ago, people could refuse to rent a one-bedroom apartment to two men. This wasn't twenty years ago; it was a handful of years ago. That marginalized community is still dealing with discrimination. Many elderly LGBTQ+ people are forced to go back in the closet in order to live in a 55+ community. It's simply too dangerous for them to be themselves around a generation of straight people who do not understand or accept them.

I am passionate about helping veterans, too, because many of them give their country years of service and then struggle to find employment when they get out of the military. I have family members who did eight years in the armed forces, got out, and had to go on food stamps because they couldn't find a job that paid enough to cover the simplest of bills.

Getting people safe places that are off the street, helping them find the mental health and support services they need, and giving them a hand up when they need it most is super important to me. To me, giving back in this way builds a stronger, better community for every single one of us.

That's a big reason why I'm have started a private equity fund, TomCo Capital Partners. It gives me the ability to rally others to invest money in ways I can't as just a contractor. I want to show people that they can help others and make money at the same time. I want to be able to give the people who need housing a safe place to lay their head at night.

And if it keeps me away from the remote and the Funyuns, I'd say that's a win-win.

If you're not doing something that makes you excited to get out of bed in the morning...then what the hell are you doing?

CHAPTER SEVENTEEN
YOU GOTTA LOVE FREE UPGRADES

"You get a lot of free stuff," my husband said to me one time as we walked up to our hotel room with extra chocolate chip cookies from the registration desk. "I'm glad I told you to do the check-in."

It's true. I almost always get a free upgrade or an extra cookie when I check into a hotel. Not because I have a handsome face or a winning smile, but because I'm nice to people.

> Most of us are just trying to do the best we can. Lighten up on others.

Some people can be really belligerent when you deal with them. Now granted, some people have jerk DNA, but in my experience, those people are almost as rare as unicorns. Most people are having a hard day or going through something. Giving them the benefit of the doubt is not only the best thing to do, it's the number-one strategy for free upgrades.

I remember meeting a woman at a conference who was rude and dismissive from the get-go. She looked a little disheveled, which came off as uncaring and disrespectful. I could have sworn off that person forever. Instead, I decided to meet with her a second time and she was a totally different person! She was the real her, not the grumpy woman I had met a few weeks earlier. After being friends with her for more than a year, I realized that 99% of the time she's an incredible person. That day, she was stressed and frustrated and she simply couldn't pull it together enough to be cordial. I get it. It happens to all of us.

> **First impressions count but second impressions tell a lot more of the story.**

When I worked in the hospitality and retail industries, I had to keep my cool no matter what. I remember one of the other associates at JC Penney came up to me. She was crying. "Can you take over for me? I don't know how to run a credit card and this customer is yelling at me."

For those boys and girls who weren't born before computers, in the old days we'd have to swipe a credit card with a carbon slip, then call the number on the back and get authorization from an actual person at the credit card company for the purchase. This associate hadn't been trained in that yet, and she was fumbling with trying to take the payment.

The customer was fuming when I came up there. After all, they'd wasted many minutes of their time just waiting for a simple credit card transaction to be processed. I was pleasant and friendly, as if the customer was smiling, not scowling. I managed to calm the situation, and by the end of the transaction, the customer apologized for being mean and impatient.

I always watch how someone treats the waiter or janitor. Their behavior tells me a lot more about them than anything else they say. You have to realize that this person, who might screw up a drink order or take a few minutes extra to process your credit card, is doing the best they can. They may have gone through some crap at home before they left for work, they might be worried about their sick kid, or they might have a mom who is being sent to hospice today.

When I worked at the resort, my friends would tell me how jealous they were. "Man, you're on the beach all day. It must be so cool." Uh, no, it's not. People working at beach restaurants and hotels aren't perfecting their tan; they are busting their asses making sure there's the right number of cherries in the daquiris.

I mentioned earlier that I tell all my clients that there will come a day when they hate me because of the disruption construction has on their lives. A few weeks ago, I was working on an elderly couple's house. They'd been waiting months for the insurance company to pay for the damage. In fact, it took them five months to get the first check—which didn't cover the full amount of damage.

They'd been promised a certain amount by the insurance company and, all of a sudden, that payment was capped and no more money was coming in. The couple had run out of money, couldn't live in their house, and one of them had to come out of retirement and go back to work just to pay the bills. For us, this was a pretty big job, a $200,000 renovation, and we had to stop work because that's not the kind of work we can afford to do pro bono.

They were already frustrated—and rightly so—and operating on a very short fuse as the renovations dragged on and on. I did everything in my power to get the insurance company to cooperate, but they refused to budge. The couple were so angry that they called the insurance company and said, "Don't pay him. He's not our contractor anymore. He stopped showing up."

Instead of throwing up my hands, I reached out to them and explained that we were a business and have to be paid so that we can pay our workers as well as purchase the necessary supplies to renovate their house. Once we talked, they calmed down. The insurance company finally sent another check so we got back to work.

I felt really bad for this couple, who were living in an aging house that had a lot of issues that weren't part of the renovation. We ended up upgrading their electrical and plumbing and throwing in a few other free upgrades before we finished the job. The insurance company still owes my company more money that we may never see; but to me, the joy on that couple's face when they were able to move back into their home was worth every penny. "Even if the insurance never pays me," I assured them, "I won't charge you. I'd rather eat those costs than make this process any more stressful."

They were thrilled. "I'm happy to be able to say I'm retired again!" the wife said. It felt good to be able to help them out and give them a bit of an upgrade to make their lives easier.

That's really the key to a free upgrade, no matter who you are—being nice to other people and showing that you genuinely care about them. They're often surprised and touched that you noticed how hard they were working. I remember the time I was on a plane with my editor, heading for Vegas. There were a few rowdy passengers on board who delayed our takeoff because they had to be escorted off the plane. I handed the flight attendants some Starbucks gift cards and told them I appreciated their patience. When the drink cart came by a little while later and I ordered some wine, the flight attendant waved off my payment. "On the house," he said.

I didn't give them the gift cards to get free wine. I did it because I know they put up with a lot of crap and deserve to have something nice done for them once in a while. It costs me almost nothing to have a few gift cards on hand to give out when I see someone struggling to do their best job in trying circumstances.

I've seen so many people judge tradespeople. "Oh, he's just a roofer," or "oh, she's just a plumber." These are the people that take care of your biggest investment, your safe place, your home. If you have a toilet that's backed up and don't know how to fix it, that plumber is an invaluable resource. Treat them like that every day of the week—not just when your toilet breaks. And keep a few gift cards on hand, just in case you want to make someone's day.

It costs very little to go the extra mile for a total stranger. Especially if you get a free drink as a thank you.

CHAPTER EIGHTEEN
SOMETIMES YOU GOTTA MAKE LEMONADE IN THE BATHTUB

When I was a little kid, maybe six or seven, I got the bright idea of setting up a lemonade stand. I'd seen it on TV and thought, "Hey, that's an easy enough way to make a lot of money, maybe even enough money to take my family to Disney World." Remember, we were poor and a trip to see Mickey was a bucket list item, not a regular occurrence.

There were, however, a few problems with that plan that my second-grade self didn't see:

- I lived in the middle of nowhere. If I was lucky, a handful of cars would go down my road in a single afternoon.
- I lived at the end of a very, very, very long driveway. Which meant carrying my supplies quite far, and I wasn't exactly Hercules.
- I had no idea what the hell I was doing.

Because I had such a long walk, and because I was incredibly optimistic about the rush of traffic for a glass of lemonade on a hot summer afternoon in Florida, I decided one measly pitcher of lemonade wouldn't be enough. What if ten customers showed up at once? I'd run out and, thus, not make money. I needed more lemonade. Lots more.

And here's where an incredible, amazing, oh-so-bright idea popped into my head: *Why not make the lemonade in the bathtub?* Then I'd have a giant batch done all at once and have plenty if a hundred people came by for lemonade. I could already see me handing the money to my parents and them shouting, "We're going to Disney World!"

I filled up the bathtub with cold water. Then I started adding scoops of powder from the yellow tub of Country Time Lemonade with its "All Natural Flavors!" And before you get all grossed out, you should know my mother came in right then and said, "What the hell are you doing with my lemonade?" She made me pull the plug on my idea and my lemonade. I was extremely disappointed that my get-rich-quick scheme had been so easily thwarted.

That was not, however, the end of my entrepreneurship aspirations. I always knew I wanted to do something that would make a lot of money, something where I was in charge of the growth of the business.

Clearly that business was not going to be lemonade stands.

I regrouped and started a small business mowing lawns, raking leaves, that kind of thing. When I got a little older, I got a job at a feed store creating digital advertisements for their newsletter. Eventually, I got my first job in retail and found out I wasn't a fan of working for somebody else.

> My parents always told me the best thing to do was get a job and work there thirty years. When you're done, the boss will reward you with a gold watch and a pension. When I became an adult, I realized that was bullshit.

Here's the cold, hard truth: There is no company out there looking to reward your years of effort. Companies are there to reward their own efforts. Plus, no one holds any job for thirty years in this day and age, and pensions are about as plentiful as dinosaurs.

All of the jobs I held before I opened my own company taught me an invaluable diversity of skills and perspectives. Those jobs also fueled me to go out on my own and grow bigger than anyone imagined possible.

When I first started out, I was the one swinging the hammer in between trying to find work, and I realized I was putting *a lot* of effort into a bunch of small jobs. That's when I had another bright idea: I needed to start looking at my business in terms of a bathtub. If I was going to grow exponentially, I needed to think beyond a single pitcher.

There's a story from 2014 about Southwest Airlines and how they were running way behind schedule all the time. They didn't know how to fix the problem. The industry standard was to call an airline consultant who would come in, tell you what you were doing wrong, and then give you tips on how to get your planes out of the gates on time.

But Southwest wanted someone who would think about the problem in a new way. Maybe the tried-and-true methods of the airline industry weren't the best for a little upstart airline with a bad scheduling track record.

They called NASCAR. Yep, the same people who can get a vehicle in and out of a pitstop with gas, oil, and four new tires in less than nine seconds. With the help of these out-of-the-airline-box thinkers, Southwest reduced their turnaround time from 55 minutes to 15.[2] That helped them become a

---

2 https://rickdacri.wordpress.com/2011/06/03/creative-problem-solving-innovation-nascar-pit-crews/

leader in the industry and, for a while, the number-one airline in the country.[3]

I was fascinated by this idea. Southwest refused to do the same thing the way everyone else had, and it paid off well for them. Then it occurred to me—why did I have to do things the same way everyone else was?

For most contractors, you knock on doors, advertise what you do, and sell your service, very often to investors who are doing multiple projects at one time. The investors are putting up the capital, but the contractor is doing all the work. Yes, you're getting paid, but there's someone else behind you who is making 20 or 30% of the project price just for putting it together.

Why couldn't I be the source of that money instead? Then we could fund our own projects, which meant we could do more jobs and make more money, but charge less because we cut out the middle man.

Right then and there, I decided to form my own capital company.

A lot of people probably thought was crazy. Stay in your lane, they tell me. Why do you want to get involved in that?

Because I'm thinking bathtubs, not pitchers. By being able to do five times as much work, I can grow that much faster

---

[3] https://www.nerdwallet.com/article/travel/is-southwest-airlines-good

and have the capital to put into my passion projects, like affordable housing. When you start thinking about growing by economies of scale, it becomes exponentially easier to do the bigger you get.

I had bathtub thinking for the launch of this book. I wasn't going to just have a little party with a few friends and some canapés. I decided to do a multi-day summit, called the Building Success Summit, where we would partner with multiple other companies to bring in investor opportunities, networking on steroids, a charity fundraiser, and a fun party at the end. Oh yeah, and you'll be able to get my book, too.

Now I have a large group of people on board, all assisting with this project. They have a vested interest in it, which mitigates the risk but also spreads the wealth of opportunities to all. Succeeding on my own is great, but succeeding with others is even better.

There's no rule declaring your business or your future has to be the same as everyone else's. There's no rule saying that a book launch has to be a small, boring event. There's no rule saying a business summit has to be a dull, dry event. Why not make both of those bigger and more fun? Why not throw in some yachts, a few drag queens, and all kinds of other crazy stuff?

Sorry to say, there won't be a bathtub there, but there will definitely be a lot of people thinking in terms of bathtubs, not pitchers.

Building success by yourself is no fun. Building success with other people...well, that's a party!

CHAPTER NINETEEN
32 BOXES OF M&M'S IS EXACTLY ENOUGH

In the olden days, kids—meaning before everything in the world was connected to the Internet—the guy who filled the vending machines at rest areas and in hospitals had to go around with boxes and boxes of inventory in the back of his truck. Before he left the warehouse, he'd make his best guesstimate about how many packages of M&M's he'd need and how many sticks of Doublemint sold the week prior. If there'd been a sudden run on Doritos the week before at the Polk County Rest Area, he wouldn't have enough to restock the machine.

Then there'd be a lot of unhappy Dorito lovers in Polk County.

A few months ago, I was at a networking event where I met a guy named Mike. I asked him what he did and he said, "Vending machine distribution."

This is where lots of people would say, "Nice to meet you," and be on their way. After all, Nothing my business does has anything to do with vending machines. This guy was not a connection for me in any way, but I like to learn about other people and what they do. You never know where there's going to be an invaluable lesson.

We started chatting about our respective industries. I told him about the vending machines I saw in my son's school and about seeing the trucks on the roads back in the day. "Well, you know," Mike said, "all the vending machines are smart now."

Meaning, today's vending machines are Wi-Fi-enabled and smart enough to know when their inventory is low. They connect to the internet, and then to the payment system, and finally to the distribution center. Kids can pay for their snacks with debit cards or QR codes that link to their Venmo apps, and restockers get just-in-time inventory reports on the status of each and every vending machine.

He told me that the machines can hold, in general, fifty of each product. If the Polk County Rest Area vending machine sells a bunch of M&M's that week, the distribution center gets a report saying there are only eighteen packages left. They'll run a report like that for every machine on the driver's route so that he knows exactly how many bags of Doritos and boxes of M&M's he needs.

It's a brilliant concept. It reduces the amount of inventory needed in the warehouse. Cuts down on loading and unloading time for the trucks. Keeps the vending machines stocked before there are unhappy Doritos lovers on I-4.

> Technology can save you time, effort, and most of all, money. If you're not taking advantage of those benefits, your business will eventually suffer.

That got me thinking about construction and how I could use technology to make every job more efficient. One of the first things we did to use technology in a new way was invest in a 3-D modeling camera. We can walk through a site, take all the images and measurements, and use that to go through the plan with a client virtually. It also helps us to put together a more accurate estimate of the work, so when the client decides to add a closet here or take down a wall there, we don't have to go back and forth to the job site to remeasure. The scanner puts the data into our design software and helps us enormously to create an accurate design.

I'm constantly thinking about how else I can use technology to improve my business. For instance, when the guys leave for the day, it would be great to have some kind of system that tells them exactly which tools and supplies they need so they can load their trucks with everything for that job. I'd love to see every tool outfitted with an RFID tag so the crew gets in the truck, hits a button, and realizes the hammer was left on the job site.

I don't have RFID tags for the tools my crews use (yet; but reach out to me if you're the developer of such a system) but I love that a simple conversation with someone I seemingly had nothing in common with led to more out-of-the-box thinking for me.

Until we have those tags, there are rubrics, ones every business owner should use. As I mentioned earlier in the book, you have to know your numbers. Have some kind of standard that you check on a regular basis because that gives you predictive ability and will tell you exactly where to put your efforts.

That way, you're not showing up at the job site with a thousand bags of Doritos when you only needed a case of M&M's. Be as smart as a vending machine and it'll make your bottom line that much better.

Be an interesting person, meet interesting people, and you'll learn interesting things. Be a boring person and no one will want to meet you, and you won't learn a damned thing.

CHAPTER TWENTY
GREEN IS THE COLOR OF DISRUPTORS

In a sea of 8,000,000,000 people in the world, it can be tough to stand out. Even in a crowd of two hundred people, making enough of an impression that someone remembers you years later is no easy feat.

Unless you're not afraid to wear something a little…different from what people would expect.

For me, that something was a green hardhat, the same green hardhat you see in the pictures of me in this book, on my website, and on my social media. Almost by accident, that hardhat became my signature.

In 2019, I decided to get my LGBT Business Enterprise certification. A few months later, the National Gay and

Lesbian Chamber of Commerce held their annual conference here in Tampa. I'd been to events that size before and knew it would be one big mishmash of nametags and suit jackets.

How was I going to stand out? How was I going to be the contractor they remembered?

There aren't many construction people in the organization (or in many of the Chambers of Commerce I've visited), but just putting "Contractor" on my nametag wasn't going to make me any more memorable than the bruschetta. I wanted an easy-to-get visual that would immediately make people associate my face with construction.

I didn't want to look like the maintenance guy coming to work on the roof, so I bought a green hardhat instead of a yellow one. I attached some rainbow temporary tattoos on the side of the hard hat. They were small, a subtle message that I was definitely an LGBTQ+-friendly company.

It was a professional event, which meant wearing a suit, but that didn't mean every inch of my suit had to be boring. I found a tie that was covered in a blueprint pattern and, when paired with the hardhat, it was pretty clear who and what I was.

I stood out in a crowd, to be sure. The national organization was filming a story about the event and I was one of the few people they interviewed, simply because you could see me from a mile away. That interview is still on their website, all these years later.

I took a break from conferences for a little bit (Covid), but went to the national conference in Denver in 2023. I wore the same hard hat with a different suit and tie.

Almost as soon as I walked into the room, two of the head procurement officers from JPMorgan Chase came up to me. "I remember you," they said. "We had a great conversation about construction at the Tampa event." Even though we'd only spoken for a few minutes four years ago, they remembered me, the conversation, and the hardhat.

"Wow, really?" I was stunned.

"Remember how we took a selfie with you that day because we loved the hardhat so much?" one of the other men said. "That picture went out in our company-wide newsletter. All of JPMorgan Chase saw your hardhat."

Such a simple decision on my part had a long-term, resonating effect on so many people and got me several high-level meetings with people I never would have met otherwise. In a room full of suits, you have no idea which people work in the construction industry—unless they're advertising their business with a hardhat. "Remember the green hardhat guy?" someone will say. "That's Tommy, with TomCo Solutions."

I love being the different one, the person who thinks outside the box and does things someone else might *not*. I didn't set out to be a disruptor, but I think that tendency has been in me since childhood. I was always an outlier in school; not exactly "that weird kid," but the one who sat on the fringe of the social cliques. After high school, I was the person who'd say aloud what everyone else was thinking but didn't dare speak. I learned to embrace what made me different from the rest and to stop being afraid what other people thought.

Case in point: I remember being at a homeowner's association conference. Most of the attendees were in classes, which left the vendor hall pretty empty and insanely boring. If you've ever been to one of those things, you know the vendors are focused on sales and there's not a lot of fun to be had.

I started trading jokes with the employee who was manning my booth with me. Pretty soon we were laughing our asses off. Other vendors wandered over to our booth, intrigued and wanting to join in on the fun (have I mentioned those conferences are boring?). I wasn't doing anything unique; I was just being me…and maybe being a little disruptive. This was the first time I felt like I was sitting at the popular kids' lunch table.

> Being yourself is the very best thing you can be.

When my company was struggling after Covid, I realized pretty quickly that it's exhausting to constantly be knocking on doors, posting on social media, and trying to sell your services while hopping from job to job. The idea of decades of doing that and hoping my business somehow took off seemed like torture.

That wasn't the life I wanted. But to get to a different life meant I had to do things differently. *Think* differently.

Instead of climbing the same steps as every other construction company in the world, I decided to look at the way multi-million-dollar companies worked. They have PR companies and marketing firms who spread the word about what they do. They invest across a broad spectrum of industries and are constantly looking forward, not just at the present day.

Just like that, serendipity happened. While I was attending a membership event at the Tampa Club, I met Alexis Quintal. She ran a small PR firm in Tampa. I started asking her questions, and she explained that public relations has evolved far beyond the occasional new hire press release. It's about building a personal brand and communicating a message about what that brand represents. I realized I might not be able to do everything the big guys are doing, but I could afford to do one thing, like hiring her PR firm.

The cost to hire her wasn't cheap, but it also wasn't as expensive as I thought. In the beginning, setting aside the money for PR strained my resources a little. But I knew making that investment would work toward a much bigger goal. Before I knew it, people started to recognize me (even without my hardhat on). I was invited to speak at a variety of events, was featured on the news, and saw my social media reach grow. I wasn't trying hard to make an impression or even get a referral; I was simply being myself.

On LinkedIn, I chronicled many of these events and adventures as part of "Tommy's Travels." There was no sales agenda involved when I did something like talk about the great day I had at the Florida Aquarium. I was simply letting people have a peek into who I am as a person and building those key cornerstones of know, like, trust.

Was it uncomfortable at first? Hell yes. I'm not a social media expert, don't have a background in TV or photography, and had no idea how to pose or do a quick promo video. But I kept doing those uncomfortable things until they got comfortable and, *boom!*, being asked for an interview by a TV reporter became NBD.

> If you're uncomfortable doing something, that's probably a sign you should keep doing it until it becomes second nature. Nobody gets to the top by staying stuck in the same old rut.

The more experiences like that I had, the more I realized I'm not a sales guy. I can close a deal, but my heart really lies in connecting, learning, and growing. Working in a wide variety of industries has given me a diverse set of skills, all of which I've brought to my own business. Choosing to get to know people who might never give me a referral or hire me has meant I've learned a lot of interesting things that I've been able to apply to TomCo. Admitting my fears and doubts to others has given them the freedom and safe space to open up about their own, which just plain makes the world a better place.

For example, I was a nervous wreck the first time I hosted my podcast. When a guest comes in and is sweating bullets and staring at the mic like it might bite, I tell them how terrified I was when I first started recording. It sets them at ease and lets them know we're all in this together.

Being open to new experiences and new avenues has also brought me down some interesting paths. For instance, a start-up AI company in Tampa approached me because they'd seen some of what I'd posted and wanted my help with operations. They were doing incredible things with Artificial Intelligence, so we talked about them adding a construction product that tied in with estimating and job costing. Yes, it's a new way of working the numbers for construction, and I think that's awesome.

Part of what I'm looking to do to help TomCo Solutions grow is to acquire other construction businesses. This is an industry battling a growing shortage of trained professionals. A massive number of people in construction will be retiring soon, which means a massive number of construction businesses will be going up for sale.

Not everyone has the licenses, skill, desire, or funds to buy those businesses and keep them running. For me, I see this as an unprecedented opportunity to grow my construction company, not by knocking on doors but by acquiring other companies and raising them to a new level by applying all the lessons I have learned. I don't want to see companies others worked their lives to build die and be forgotten. I want them to become part of a bigger future where we're building homes that give every single human being a safe place to lay their head at night.

There are going to be things that stump me and obstacles that get in my way. No problem. If I don't know how to do something, I find the people who do. I don't have to be an expert in any of those things because there are plenty of incredible people out there who already have that expertise.

I don't understand the way the algorithms and video editing works, so I hired a social media company to help me build my presence on channels like TikTok and Instagram. I had no idea how to write a book when I started *Building Success*, so I hired an editor who'd make me look amazing on paper.

When I first told people I was writing a book, they asked me if it would be about construction or real estate. The last thing the world needs, I told them, is another book about those topics from yet another contractor. I want to talk about overcoming adversity, conquering challenges, taking risks, embracing failure, and rethinking the definition of success.

That is valuable information to people because we all have dreams. We've all had setbacks. We're all seeking inspiration for when times get tough. When they hear or read about someone who has gone through the tough times and not only made it back but made it back even stronger, they think, *"Maybe I can do that, too."*

Because that's what I thought when I read other people's books about those topics. Those were the people who inspired me, who made me see the future as limitless.

It's humbling when people come up to me and say they were inspired by my story. I haven't written the last chapter of my life or my business, so there's a good chance there will be another book in the future. Make sure to leave some room on your bookshelves.

In the meantime, I'm going to keep doing things some folks might call disruptive. Like hosting a multi-day business summit along with my book launch. Like building affordable housing for underserved communities. Like someday opening a trade school to encourage young people to get into this industry. Like telling a joke in a crowded room just so things are a little less boring and we all get to know each other just a little more.

I don't want to build success just for me. I want to build it for you, and for that person over there, the one whose looking over your shoulder and dreaming of someday being in your shoes. After all, it takes a lot more than a single piece of wood to create a home, and it takes a lot more than a single person to build a future that embraces us all.

Be kind, be generous, be yourself, and don't be afraid to be a little disruptive...and you'll always be successful.

PHOTO ALBUM

Left to Right: Nathan, Matthew, & Tommy - 2023

Left to Right: Matthew, Grandma, & Nathan

Nathan & Tommy

Nathan, Mom, & Tommy

Emma

Edgar

Tommy & Gary

Tiffany (Sister) & Tommy

Matthew (Son), Aidan (Nephew), Grandma, & Rylan (Nephew)

Nathan, Lois (Nathan's Mom), Mary Poppins, Grandma, & Tommy

Me and my editor, Shirley Jump

ACKNOWLEDGMENTS

I am profoundly grateful to a constellation of remarkable individuals whose support, love, and guidance illuminated the journey of writing this book.

Firstly, to my husband, Nathan, whose unwavering faith in me provided the strength to pursue this dream. Your patience and love are the bedrock on which I stand. To our son, Matthew, who brings endless joy and inspiration into our lives, thank you for your understanding and for the laughter that filled our home during the most demanding days. And to our fur babies, Emma and Edgar, for their constant purrs of support.

My sister, Tiffany, and my nephews, Aidan and Ryan, your encouragement and belief in my work have been invaluable. Your support has been a source of comfort and motivation, reminding me of the importance of family bonds in nurturing creativity.

To my beloved grandmother, whose wisdom and stories have always been a source of inspiration and comfort. You have instilled in me the values of persistence and grace under pressure. Your love and support have been my guiding light, and I carry your strength with me in every word I write.

Building off the dedication to my mother, I want to extend a special acknowledgement here to her as well. Mom, your indomitable spirit and love have shaped me in ways beyond words. This book, while a reflection of my journey, is imbued with the lessons of resilience and love you've instilled in me. Your legacy is woven into the fabric of my life and this story. Thank you for being my first and most enduring inspiration.

A special acknowledgment to Marleta Black, who not only penned the forward, offering readers a warm entrance into this journey, but also stood by me as an incredible advisor and source of encouragement throughout the writing process. Marleta, your guidance, drawn from your experience as a published author, was invaluable. Your belief in my story has been a beacon of support, for which I am eternally grateful.

To my team at TomCo Solutions: Matt Klaus and Zach Gerbholz, Matt Klaus, Zach Gerbholz, Valerie St. Marin, Ryan Listerman, and Brandie Adams, thank you for your unyielding support and for the countless ways you've contributed to both my personal growth and professional achievements. Your dedication, creativity, and enthusiasm have been a source of strength and inspiration throughout this journey.

A heartfelt acknowledgement to my communications team, who have played a pivotal role in helping me stand out: Alexis Quintal of Rosarium PR & Marketing, Maureen Famiano of

ACKNOWLEDGMENTS

MEFMedia, and Matt Dzierbun of 4EDGE. Your expertise, vision, and dedication to excellence have been instrumental in bringing my voice to a broader audience. Thank you for your strategic guidance and for believing in the power of this story.

A heartfelt thank you to Shirley Jump, my editor, whose expertise and insight transformed my vision into reality. I would never have been able to do this on my own. Shirley, your patience, skill, and dedication are unparalleled. Working with you has been a privilege, and I could not have wished for a better guide through this process.

A heartfelt thank you to my incredible friend, Jessica Casucci, who embraces me as a "Space Sibling" with genuine warmth and affection. Your thoughtful interviews and the special audio content you created for this book have added a unique and cherished dimension to this project.

Thank you to Ann and Edward Pereira for the incredible connections, collaborations, and good times that you have provided. Your support and friendship have enriched this journey in countless ways.

My deepest gratitude to The Tampa Club and its amazing staff for fostering a vibrant and welcoming atmosphere that seamlessly blends business with pleasure. Your dedication and warmth have made every visit an enriching experience. Special thanks to Tim, Alissa, Erin, Sherry, Justin, Lauren, Thomas, James, Crystal, Tangie, Jake, Rebekah, and all the rest for your exceptional service and hospitality.

To my best friend of over twenty years, Gary Carlson, who has been there through every high and low. Gary, your friendship is a treasure, and your support has been a pillar of strength for me. Your belief in my work has been a constant source of encouragement.

A special thank you goes out to the countless books and authors that have inspired me over the years. Your stories have fueled my imagination and taught me the power of words.

And finally, to anyone who has ever encouraged a dream, offered a kind word, or lent an ear during this journey, thank you. This book is not just a product of my effort but a testament to the love and support of those around me.

Tommy

ABOUT THE AUTHOR

When Tommy Whitehead was born in 1984 in the Winter Haven, FL, hospital, he wasn't breathing.

The medical team at this small local hospital got him stabilized and quickly transferred him to Tampa General Hospital where he made a full recovery. And definitely found his voice.

Tommy's young parents struggled financially, but despite these economically challenging times, Tommy developed a robust sense of adventure and a profound love for science and technology at a young age.

A gifted student, Tommy graduated from high school at the age of sixteen, all while working a retail job to help support his family. He earned his Associate's degree in 2005 from the University of South Florida in Tampa. In 2007, Tommy married and welcomed his only child, Matthew in 2009. Following a divorce, he remarried his current spouse, Nathan, in 2018.

Tommy's career has been characterized by a voracious appetite for knowledge, gaining diverse experiences across multiple sectors including retail, law, hospitality, accounting, real estate, and construction. This eclectic background fueled his innovative approach to business. Tommy prides himself as a connector who takes an interest in a wide variety of diverging sectors.

When his mother was diagnosed with cancer in 2020 and passed away two years later, that tragic event served as a turning point for Tommy, prompting him to dedicate significant efforts towards community service and adopt a transformative approach in his professional endeavors. He has since redefined his business practices at TomCo Solutions, positioning the company as a disruptor in the construction industry. Additionally, Tommy hosts "Tommy's Toolbox – The Podcast," which delves into innovative trends in construction, technology, real estate development, and entrepreneurship.

He is also the founder of The Pride Construction Coalition, a nonprofit organization which aims to challenge and change the stigma associated with LGBTQ+ individuals in the construction sector. Furthermore, as a co-founder of a start-up AI company, Tommy is at the forefront of integrating artificial intelligence into construction processes. His latest venture, TomCo Capital Partners, focuses on fundraising for diverse

ABOUT THE AUTHOR

real estate and construction projects ranging from affordable housing to build-to-rent initiatives.

Tommy resides in the Greater Tampa Bay Area with his husband and their son Matthew. He continues to look for bigger and better ways to impact his community and the industry he loves.

For more information or to reach out to Tommy, visit tommywhitehead.com.

We would like to extend our heartfelt gratitude to Sunburst Yacht Charters for their generous support of the Building Success Conference. Your partnership has been invaluable in making this book launch event a memorable and impactful experience for all attendees. Thank you for your unwavering commitment to our mission and for helping us sail towards success!

sunburstyachtcharters.com

www.ingramcontent.com/pod-product-compliance
Lightning Source LLC
LaVergne TN
LVHW010325070526
838199LV00065B/5648